Brokenness Restored

Brokenness Restored

The Path to Recovery Is a Healing Journey

Janna Herron

Foreword by Kristin Williams

RESOURCE *Publications* · Eugene, Oregon

Resource Publications
An Imprint of Wipf and Stock Publishers
199 W. 8th Ave., Suite 3
Eugene, OR 97401

www.wipfandstock.com

PAPERBACK ISBN: 979-8-3852-6595-4
HARDCOVER ISBN: 979-8-3852-6596-1
EBOOK ISBN: 979-8-3852-6597-8
VERSION NUMBER 01/07/26

This book is written as a source of information only. The information contained in this book should not be considered a substitute for the advice, decisions, or judgment of the reader's physician or other professional advisors.

Some personal names and identifying details have been changed to protect the privacy of the individuals involved.

This book is dedicated to the support system that God has blessed me with. You all hold a special place in my heart, having been with me through reoccurring trials and tribulations, holding me in the depths of my brokenness, and always pointing me to the hope that we have in Christ Jesus. I shall be forever grateful.

Contents

Foreword by Kristin Williams | ix

Introduction | xi

Chapter 1: Surviving, Not Thriving | 1

Chapter 2: Distrusting the World | 10

Chapter 3: Facing Reality | 19

Chapter 4: Honesty Is Best | 29

Chapter 5: Desperation in Darkness | 38

Chapter 6: Breaking Trust | 48

Chapter 7: Defiant Fear | 58

Chapter 8: Over-Compliant Fear | 68

Chapter 9: Resurfaced Suppression | 77

Chapter 10: Broken Beyond Repair | 89

Chapter 11: Hitting Rock Bottom | 98

Chapter 12: God Uses the Broken | 109

Acknowledgments | 119

Foreword

BROKENNESS RESTORED IS A raw, vulnerable, and transparent story of a young woman finding unexpected joy through desperate dependence on Jesus. Within the pages of her book, Janna shares such an honest reflection of her testimony that will leave readers assured that they are not alone in their struggles. Janna's story is one that is constantly pointing back to the goodness of God, His closeness to the brokenhearted and His unending mercies.

In a world that focuses on being the hero of your own story, Janna relentlessly points us back to the only one who can really heal us, Jesus Christ. She reminds us that, as broken humans, we don't have the power to save ourselves and that's good news because it means we can stop striving! True and sustainable behavior change starts with a transformed heart and a deep understanding of our infinite worth. This is a story of courage, persistence, and faith in the transformative work of God.

It just takes one courageous woman willing to stand up and share her story in order that others may then feel empowered to do the same. You see, the enemy wants us isolated. He wants us to believe that we are the only ones struggling and he wants to convince us that it would be too shameful to share our burdens with anyone else. But like a metastasizing cancer, our struggles are only intensified in isolation.

When a woman is willing to stand up and share her story with vulnerability and transparency, chains begin to break. Walls begin to fall. Others begin to realize that they are not alone and start reaching out for support. Women begin praying for one another, speaking truth in love and holding each other accountable. This is how we wrestle well as a community of believers, willing to pull our messy lives out of the darkness and choose healing over hiding.

Brokenness Restored is a courageous woman's story put to paper as Janna's brave declaration of, "I'll go first." In her openness and willingness to share her own testimony, Janna is inviting readers to do the same. My hope and prayers are that as you read this book, you would feel deeply seen and understood in parts of your own story and that your heart would slowly be transformed with the turning of each page.

I hope that, by the last chapter, you feel inspired to share your personal testimony with someone safe and that you are empowered to seek support if needed.

In a culture full of filtered images, edited stories and unrealistic expectations, Janna's real and honest testimony is not only refreshing, but also a powerful reminder of the goodness of God and the hope that we have in Him. The hope that is an anchor for our souls (Hebrews 6:19).

We serve a God who makes beauty from ashes. A God who can call out dry bones to come alive. A God who can make a masterpiece out of our mess.

Truly there is hope within the broken.

Kristin Williams
RDN, LD, CEDS
and author of *Unworthy Weight*

Introduction

ANXIETY IS THAT ANNOYING friend who won't stop talking for a second so that I can get a word in to ask what their purpose is. Anger is that direct friend who isn't afraid to blame me and confront my behavior, becoming a harsh inner critic. Fear is that doubtful friend that makes my mind spiral and spin in more ways than I can count . . . and depression is that lonely friend that leaves me isolated and left in a pit of despair and darkness where I've forgotten the hope that I have in Jesus. When have negative emotions caused you to doubt or forget the hope that God gives us in this life?

As I share my story of brokenness and spiritual warfare in the depths of mental illness, I point to the biblical truth that God has revealed to me on my healing journey. However, it does not end there because the healing journey is lifelong!

May this be the start of a light at the end of the tunnel for those that find themselves trapped in the darkness. May the scripture provided in this book encourage you and point you to the One who brings hope and peace amidst chaos. May you find freedom in embracing Jesus and surrendering your whole heart to Him to begin your own journey of healing. May God use my story to speak to your heart.

I share my brokenness with you to show you just how POWERFUL our God is.

I share my darkness with you to show you that God is LIGHT.

I share my regrets with you to show you how FORGIVING our God is.

I share my shame with you to show you the GRACE of our God.

I share my rock-bottom moments with you to show you the depth of God's LOVE.

If God never gave up on me and pursued and comforted me in my darkness . . . I whole-heartedly believe that He will do the same for you. You are never alone. It may feel like it at times . . . BUT God tells us not to fear and promises that He will never leave nor forsake us in Deuteronomy 31:6.

As you read my story, I encourage you to highlight the Bible verses and biblical truths, to ponder the questions at the end of each chapter, to think about how mental illness impacts our world, to reflect on how God has shown up in your life, and to ultimately give God glory for the hope that we have in Christ Jesus, even amidst the brokenness inside.

Rejoice that He has covered us with His blood and that we are washed white!

Rejoice that we are made new and have freedom in Christ!

Rejoice that we have hope inside!

Chapter 1

Surviving, Not Thriving

I WAS FREE.

I mean . . . I was an 18-year-old, high school valedictorian that just moved into a college dorm for the fall semester of 2018, with the freedom to do absolutely whatever I wanted to. I barely had contact with my parents and I was all about my friends. I was a music therapy major that did not actually know what I wanted to do with my life.

I worked on campus as a student assistant for the Department of Teacher Education and had many other odd jobs like babysitting, pet sitting, and being a piano accompanist for various occasions. I thought that I had everything together. After all, I had moved out of my abusive childhood home, and I honestly believed that I could just forget my traumatic childhood even happened.

Unfortunately, it doesn't work that way.

My entire childhood, I threw myself into people-pleasing and perfectionism because I honestly believed that the abuse at home would stop if I was "perfect" enough. I quickly learned that this was not the case, but I still pushed myself to excel in every area because it helped to cover the pain. So naturally, when I went to college, I believed that I could do the same. However, when memories, thoughts, and emotions have been suppressed for long periods of time . . . they will resurface in some way. Let me repeat that.

When memories, thoughts, and emotions are suppressed for long periods of time . . . they will resurface in some way, whether you want them to or not. I can almost hear God saying,

"Sweet child, why did you not give me those memories, thoughts, and emotions? Why did you push them down, hide them, and try to go your own way?"

If I could go back in time, I would ask myself exactly that. But there I was, a freshman in college, with a full ride, continuing to throw myself at the feet of people to please and overcommit myself, desperately trying to prove that I was "perfect" in every way. I felt like I was on top of the world, having survived my abusive home, determined to never experience anything of the sort again and to prove that I never needed anyone's help. Oh, how pride overtook me, and God humbled me in a heartbeat.

When I first met my piano professor, who I had to take one on one lessons with, in addition to a group class, I thought that he was strict, but somewhat okay. However, with time, the strictness became condescending, critical, and demeaning, barreling head over heels into emotional abuse. I started crying in every private lesson, in which he would grow angry and make me play my music even as tears clouded my vision. Memories of my abusive childhood started to resurface as I continued to try and force them down.

I started to have nightmares again. I started to have flashbacks and panic attacks that left me shaking on the bathroom floor in the music hall. I remember relapsing on self-harm, restricting my food intake again to have a sense of control, and feeling so incredibly angry and disappointed in myself because I was supposed to be the girl that had everything together . . . not the girl abusing her body, hiding, and crying in a corner.

I was falling apart.

I started to blame God.

In my darkness, I spoke out of anger when I asked Him where He was all the years of my childhood. I asked Him why He let me go through what I did. I reflected on the day that Child Protective

Services showed up at my school because they were concerned, but ultimately, they apologized that I was a case that slipped through the cracks because I was about to become an adult and graduate high school.

They apologized for not being able to intervene sooner. I remember seething with anger and asking them to leave. I asked God why He did not intervene sooner. I'm sure many people have asked similar questions themselves, and you might have even asked them yourself.

As much as I wish I could have offered my younger self some comfort, at least I can offer it to you. Soloman wrote about God's timing in Ecclesiastes 3:1–8, 11.

> There is a time for everything, and a season for every activity under the heavens: a time to be born and a time to die, a time to plant and a time to uproot, a time to kill and a time to heal, a time to tear down and a time to build, a time to weep and a time to laugh, a time to mourn and a time to dance, a time to scatter stones and a time to gather them, a time to embrace and a time to refrain from embracing, a time to search and a time to give up, a time to keep and a time to throw away, a time to tear and a time to mend, a time to be silent and a time to speak, a time to love and a time to hate, a time for war and a time for peace . . . He has made everything beautiful in its time. He has also set eternity in the human heart; yet no one can fathom what God has done from beginning to end.

As scary as it may seem to release control and acknowledge that God has control over time, how blessed we are to know that "He has made everything beautiful in its time," and that He will bring beauty from ashes, as we are told in Isaiah 61:3. We may not understand why God allows times of weeping to happen. We may not understand why there are times of mourning, pain, or suffering. We may not understand why there are wars.

However, I can believe that God will turn ashes into beauty in the grand scheme of His timeline and humble myself to acknowledge that I cannot possibly fathom the extent of eternity and what the future will bring out of all the brokenness in this world.

Being human, we should know better than anyone that there are different seasons of life. There is childhood. There are college years. There is singleness. There is marriage. There is parenthood. There is career, just to name some of the main ones we think of when someone mentions walking through a certain season of life. However, I think it is too easy to get caught up in the mundane walks of life that most people experience while trying to cover up and hide the more challenging seasons. Social media is a big culprit of this.

Throughout my freshman and sophomore years of college, I desperately tried to keep my "perfect" façade up to date on my social media pages. It was evident that mostly everyone else in my life did so too. There were only ever posts about achievements and special events like award ceremonies, graduations, weddings, baby announcements, etc., where smiles and laughter flooded my social media feed. It was like living in a daydream as I scrolled constantly, comparison and envy creeping up within me. Suddenly, everything felt like competition and with the decline of my mental health, I felt like the ultimate failure, but I still tried my best to cover it up.

I posted my cutest selfies, my college adventures, my hang-out with friends, my achievements in work, church, and school. I posted my "best" self for the world to see, when I was simply faking the smiles. I'm sure many of you can relate to faking a smile or using social media as a hideout for how you are really doing in life. However, just like suppression is never the answer . . . hiding isn't either. Jesus tells us in Luke 8:17 that anything hidden will surely be revealed in time, whether you want it to or not.

> For there is nothing hidden that will not be disclosed, and nothing concealed that will not be known or brought out into the open.

This is a bit intimidating for me to acknowledge as I spent more than half my life hiding, and I certainly learned this truth. I wonder if it might be hard for you to read as well. There were times where I even thought that I could hide from God, but as Jeremiah 23:24 says,

> Who can hide in secret places so that I cannot see them? declares the LORD. "Do not I fill heaven and earth? declares the LORD.

Even Adam and Eve tried to hide from God when they sinned in the Garden of Eden, but that is a clear picture that there is no hiding from God. He sees and knows all things. It can also be seen throughout the entirety of the Bible. I don't know about you, but on my healing journey, I have learned to take comfort in knowing a God that sees and knows all things. It means that He sees all of me, accepts all of me, and loves me for me. However, it took time and healing to believe this for myself as God graciously waited for me to learn my lesson the hard way in the darkest years of my life.

In 2019, during the fall semester of my sophomore year, many things seemed to happen all at once. I was a Resident Assistant (RA) for the brand-new dorm hall on campus, which only added to my stress and trauma by having to live where I worked and attend to emergency situations. I stretched myself thin with the number of babysitting jobs I accepted on the side.

I started getting involved in too many organizations on campus and on top of all that, a campus investigation opened for the piano professor I told you about and so I got tossed into the middle of that mess. Gradually, I spiraled and inside, the darkness only seemed to grow as Post-Traumatic Stress Disorder, depression, anxiety, and Anorexia Nervosa took control.

I started to seek counseling services on campus but only let a handful of people know about it because I was still trying to hold myself together. Part of me was frustrated that I was not how I was in high school, highly involved in orchestra at both church and school, involved in majority of the clubs where I held many officer positions, babysitting an assistant principal's kids, volunteering at various places, president of the National Honor Society and piano accompanist for the top choir in senior year, and still able to ace every single International Baccalaureate (IB) class without a second thought.

If you don't know what IB is . . . it is basically a very rigorous academic program that is all research, presentation, project, volunteer, and essay-based (no multiple choice) that I will claim is even harder than college itself. With that said, you can see my frustration when my grades in college were too many B's and C's for my liking.

It was nearing finals week in this difficult semester when my counselor at that time expressed her concern for me. She mentioned that because I was self-harming, restricting my food intake, overexercising, and having increased suicidal thoughts, she thought that it would be best for me not to stay on campus over the winter break and maybe even into the next semester. In other words, the school did not want to be held liable if something were to happen to me and well . . . since my relationship with my parents was basically nonexistent . . . I panicked.

BUT God.

I didn't even ask for His help because I still harbored resentment . . . but He still provided. When I look back now, I see that God provided the right people at exactly the right time, throughout the entirety of my life. His help may not have always looked like how I wanted it to look . . . but He still provided. The Bible gives us many examples of how God has provided for His people, especially the Israelites, during their time in the wilderness.

Not only did God rescue them from Egypt, but He did these things: parted the Red Sea; protected with a pillar of cloud by day and a pillar of fire by night; provided water, manna, and quail; defeated many of their enemies; gave them the Ten Commandments so that they would be able to live long in the promised land as it says in Deuteronomy 11:8–9.

We are also told of His promise of provision in Philippians 4:19.

> And my God will meet all your needs according to the riches of his glory in Christ Jesus.

Something I have also learned throughout my journey, is that we must run from the mindset of instant gratification because more often than not, we are not going to recognize how God meets our needs until the time has passed. We are not always going to get our way at that very moment. However, in this instant, God did answer pretty immediately. It just so happens that one of my church youth group leaders that I met in high school, offered their third bedroom to me even though she was pregnant with her second child.

The timing was perfect because a few months later, Covid-19 shut everything down in the spring of 2020. Not only was I getting to experience what a Christ-centered, healthy family unit was like, but I was also not alone in a pandemic of isolation. They provided me with support when I was completely lost and treated me as part of the family . . . my heart will forever be grateful for their love, generosity, and compassion.

This time period was also one that was filled with breakdowns, nightmares, flashbacks, and tears which led to the start of my psychiatric medication journey. My family had made it clear that they did not want to acknowledge mental health struggles and would certainly not provide any financial means of getting me the help that I needed. I was devastated and hopeless.

BUT God.

The family that I was living with, just so happened to know a family friend who was a practicing psychiatrist. I was provided for financially and he took me on as a client, where I officially received the diagnosis of Post-Traumatic Stress Disorder. It was a relief to know that my struggles had a name, as much as I was worried about what other people would think if they were to ever find out about it. Little did I know that this was only the start of my journey.

The topic of psychiatric medication is a very controversial topic, especially in terms of Christianity. Many do not think of mental illness as a sickness that needs medication to be treated, even though science shows that there are actual chemical imbalances in the brain or changes to the brain structure that explain many of the symptoms experienced by those living with mental illness.

This is still the case for me, but it was very much a struggle to accept that I needed medication to help me function better in life. I felt pressure from my Asian roots to turn to herbal remedies, to simply snap out of it, or to break a generational curse. I felt pressure from the Christian world to simply have more faith, to pray more, to believe that God can heal me.

It wasn't that I did not have faith. It wasn't that I did not pray. It wasn't that I did not believe in God's miraculous healing power. I knew He could heal me because I would beg on my knees for Him to . . . but somehow . . . He chose not to, perhaps so I could stay dependent on Him for my needs.

However, He did provide me with medication. He provided me with doctors that studied for years to know how to best treat me. He provided me with treatment plans that still allow me to live a healthier life. Therefore, when I take my medication every morning and night . . . I thank God for it, and I bless it, just like I would do for the food. However, it did take many years before I found the right combination of medications that work best for me and my body.

When I was first hesitant to try medication, I was told this analogy. If someone were diagnosed with cancer and told that they needed chemotherapy for a better chance of life, would they reject the treatment? My answer was no, of course not. I was also asked, if someone had diabetes and needed insulin to live, would they reject the medication? Again, I answered of course not, in which it was explained to me that medication for mental illness is the same, because it is a treatment for a better chance at life and in severe cases, a means to live.

My psychiatrist was also a strong believer in Christ and told me that sometimes God helps us in ways that we may not want or understand. So, with that said, I gave medication a chance, and today, I can confidently say that I'm thankful God has helped me in this way.

And there I was, living with a family that accepted me for me, showed me the love of Christ, and helped me to the get the treatment that I needed. It should have been great . . . and yet I was extremely uncomfortable inside. The enemy reminded me of my past and fed me lies that I did not deserve such goodness. As we are told in 1 Peter 5:8, the devil is always lurking to use our weaknesses against us.

> Be alert and of sober mind. Your enemy the devil prowls around like a roaring lion looking for someone to devour.

He knew the reminders of my past would be my downfall. He knew that I was very weak in the mind. He tempted me to bring chaos back into my life because that was what I was used to. He made me cringe at the love and care that was given to me until I could stand it no longer.

And as a result, I moved back to the campus dorms to live alone as an RA for the summer of 2020, isolated from all I knew and loved.

I was only surviving, and I did not believe in thriving.

QUESTIONS TO THINK ABOUT

1. Is there anything you are hiding from others or God Himself? What are some steps you can take in surrendering it to God and/or letting others in?

2. What are the ways God has provided for you in your life? Can you think of moments that He provided in ways you did not necessarily want or understand?

3. Are there times in your life where you were surviving instead of thriving? Or are you in a season of surviving today?

Chapter 2

Distrusting the World

INCREDIBLY LONELY . . . THAT'S HOW I felt.

I was one of the handful of people still living in the new dorm hall for a few weeks before residents would move into an older dorm hall for the summer. I was soon to find out just how much of a mistake it was to have moved out from the family I was living with when the pandemic was still at a point of severity. If you did not already know, isolation merely increases the symptoms of depression and anxiety. So, I encourage you today that if you are finding yourself in a place of isolation or having increased feelings of loneliness . . . talk to God and reach out to others around you.

We were not meant to walk this life alone, and as it says in Ecclesiastes 4:9–12,

> Two are better than one, because they have a good return for their labor. If either of them falls down, one can help the other up. But pity anyone who falls and has no one to help them up. Also, if two lie down together, they will keep warm. But how can one keep warm alone? Though one may be overpowered, two can defend themselves. A cord of three strands is not quickly broken.

I so desperately wish that I had remembered this passage, but with time, God provided for me again, but not until I had experienced something incredibly painful and learned from it.

You could say that my distrust in the world started at a young age . . . from the moment I tried to tell teachers that I was getting bullied, but they brushed it off and told me not to tattle. From the moment I tried to express what was going on at home, but not being heard. From the moment my parents were told that I needed treatment for Anorexia at age 12, but not receiving the help that I needed. From all the moments I heard my father talk about his distrust in the world as a correctional officer in the prison system, and how he saw the brokenness of this earth, up close and personal.

If anyone worked for over 40 years in a prison system, I can't even begin to imagine what that does to a person internally. I can't blame my father for not knowing love and being able to hold onto any sort of optimism when all he experienced was hate and negativity. I can't blame him for how he had difficulty setting boundaries between work and life when he spent majority of his time in a horrific work environment. I can't blame him for how he reacted and treated us at home when he was not given a healthy example. He too, had an abusive background from his own father.

Of course, I don't overlook the pain and hurt that he has caused . . . but because God is forgiving and merciful and gracious . . . over time, I learned to let go of the anger and resentment towards him, to forgive, and to understand that I can still love him from afar, even if we do not have a relationship. This was not an easy place to get to, but I am here to tell you that it is possible to forgive even your worst enemy or the person who has hurt you the most in life . . . but only by the grace of God. We are reminded throughout the Bible of forgiveness and in Colossians 3:13, it says,

> Bear with each other and forgive one another if any of you has a grievance against someone. Forgive as the Lord forgave you.

Because we have the forgiveness of Christ, we too can forgive others, especially if we rely on God and pray daily for the heart of forgiveness.

I think something that is often misunderstood is that forgiveness means forgetting the grievances against us or fixing a relationship as if nothing had ever happened. However, forgiveness is not for the other person . . . it is actually, for you. Resentment, hurts, and pain can tear up the heart inside, but when you release that to God and replace it with forgiveness and love, it is so incredibly freeing!

There may be times when you can try to forget what has happened to you, but ultimately, we are still human, and memories linger in our minds. There may also be times when you may decide to fix a relationship, however, it will never be the exact same as it was before, and sometimes a relationship may need to be separated or cut off in protection of one's own heart and mind. At the end of the day, pray about how God wants you to respond and for your decisions to draw you closer to Him in these moments.

So, as my distrust in the world started at a young age, naturally, that distrust only continued to grow. At the age of 14, I developed a distrust specifically, in men. Upon experiencing a shocking and terrifying experience of sexual harassment in a movie theater by a senior at another high school, I started to think that all men were the same because I also thought of my father.

That encounter did not end there as the guy continued to stalk and attempt to control me even though we were clearly not in a relationship. Thankfully, he graduated high school and left, however, it already started my avoidance of men. I slowly distanced myself from friends that were guys and spoke less and less to male teachers while avoiding contact with men in public. It also influenced my decision to go to a college, primarily for women.

That is how I ended up at Texas Woman's University where I thought I would be safe, but I soon started to think that I would never be safe anywhere in this world no matter how hard I tried to be. That summer of 2020 that I lived alone, I was walking through the parking lot to get back to my dorm room when I checked over my shoulder for probably the 20th time. I was already used to being hypervigilant and would check behind me or my surroundings far too often.

Usually, it was my own mind tricking me into fear . . . however, this time my instincts were right. That night, I was followed in by a complete stranger because the locking mechanism on the dorm hall door was broken and had not yet been fixed. My worst nightmare happened when I was raped . . . and I tell my therapists today, that my dad broke me . . . but this man shattered me.

Even as a child, I knew what the Bible said about relationships, and I held onto my values dearly and very seriously. In the 4th grade, there was a boy that wanted to kiss me, but I rejected him outright because I knew that I wanted to save kissing for the right person. As I grew older, I also knew that I wanted to save sex for marriage, and I wanted to stay as pure as possible.

It was heartbreaking and shameful for me when I experienced sexual harassment as a teenager, but when I was raped at 20 . . . the shame became so overpowering that I fell into extreme body hate, not even feeling like I could live in my own body anymore. I scrubbed vigorously at my skin as I showered, over and over and over again. I washed my bed sheets, clothes, and towels too many times to count. On repeat.

I felt so incredibly shameful and guilty about what I would have to tell my future husband one day. I did not leave my room for an entire week and had ignored my phone until friends became overly concerned. I was trying even harder to push everyone away and desperately trying to isolate myself.

BUT God.

He did not let me.

One of my friends dropped by to check on me and I became an emotional mess. They convinced me to go to the doctor. I fell into a deep depression mixed with severe bouts of anxiety to even go out in public. However, to help combat this, I started working at a local Christian camp because I was not necessarily in public, per say, but I was enclosed on a campus and working with children. Even if I did not completely feel safe, I did feel like I was escaping from the world into a childlike reality.

And yet, just like there are seasons in life . . . the summer season came to an end, and I had to return to campus for another year as an RA. I was frozen with fear about the number of people I would encounter because I had become very self-conscious about my body. I was not even able to look in the mirror anymore. I knew that I had to find a way to cope, and so I did the only thing I could think of. I reverted to how I coped in childhood . . . people-pleasing and perfectionism. I started saying yes to every single commitment and opportunity I could get my hands on to try to suppress and numb the pain I felt inside. I overworked myself by balancing 15 credit hours for school and working 4 part-time jobs in addition to being an RA which was already a 24/7 job.

If you are wondering how that was possible . . . it was because I worked odd hours during various weekdays as a Sensory Motor & Cognitive Skills Coach for children with sensory processing disorders, and squeezed in as many babysitting and pet sitting jobs that I could, in addition to as much piano accompanying for church and schools, while also working various weekends at the camp I worked at during the summer. Crazy, right? Looking back on it now, it is no wonder why I fell apart.

The exhaustion crept up slowly at first, not just from sleep deprivation and overworking, but from suppressing my thoughts and feelings. At this point, I began wondering how long I could go on for, because I was starting to dread everything that I was doing. I had to drag myself out of bed each morning for a workout routine I forced myself to do. I had to speedwalk across campus, just to get to class, only to almost fall asleep several times. I started to work mindlessly at my jobs, even making mistakes here and there. It was not long before I felt fully exhausted, unable to carry on.

Even in my Christian Walk, I was no longer living out God's will for my life because I told Him that I could handle it on my own. I was still angry with Him, especially for the most recent traumatic event months prior. I became a Sunday Christian that led worship for the first service, hid in the music room until the second service that I would also lead, and then leave early because I probably had piles of homework to catch up on or another job to run to. I would still attend the college service on Tuesday nights, but I never felt like I was truly there. In other words, I became a hearer of the word instead of a doer, as it says in James 1:22–25. Even if I was leading worship, I will admit that my heart was not truly there for it at the time.

> Do not merely listen to the word, and so deceive your-selves. Do what it says. Anyone who listens to the word but does not do what it says is like someone who looks at his face in a mirror and, after looking at himself, goes away and immediately forgets what he looks like. But whoever looks intently into the perfect law that gives freedom, and continues in it—not forgetting what they have heard, but doing it—they will be blessed in what they do.

Therefore, not only did I harbor distrust for the world, but I held onto distrust in every aspect of my life, including God. Something I want to touch on for the moment, is that fact that your feelings of distrust are extremely valid. It is hard to trust, and as believers, it is actually better that we do not trust the world for what it is. The Bible tells us to not love the world in 1 John 2:15–16 and that everything in the world is not of God.

> Do not love the world or anything in the world. If anyone loves the world, love for the Father is not in them. For everything in the world—the lust of the flesh, the lust of the eyes, and the pride of life—comes not from the Father but from the world.

We must therefore guard our hearts and look to God above and not the things of this world, meaning we should have distrust in the world because it could lead us astray. However, your distrust in the world should not keep you in bondage of fear because God does not give us a spirit of fear as we are told in 2 Timothy 1:7.

> For God gave us a spirit not of fear but of power and love and self-control. (ESV)

It is so reassuring to me when I'm reminded that fear does not come from God, but from the enemy. Did you know that the words "Do not fear . . ." are said 365 times in the Bible, supporting the truth that God does not desire for us to have a spirit of fear? Over the years, I have been learning that even though I distrust the world, the one thing that I should not distrust is God Himself, and this is still a work in progress.

I think that it is natural for humans to have doubts and to ask questions. Even the disciples of Jesus had moments of doubt in the Bible. For example, in the story of Jesus walking on water in Matthew 14:22–33, Peter walks on water to reach Jesus and all is well as he focuses on the face of his teacher, until he is distracted by the waves and the wind. As his focus shifts and fear seizes him, he starts to sink, and he frantically asks for Jesus to save him. When Jesus caught him in verse 31, He says,

> You of little faith. . .why did you doubt?

I can imagine how hard it must be to hear that, but I am humbled when I put myself in Peter's shoes and think about what I would have done. I honestly would have doubted too, or I would have been shocked in disbelief. What a great moment it was for Jesus to teach the importance of keeping our eyes on God, rather than the storms in life and the distractions of the world. So, as natural as it is for humans to doubt, even as a disciple, I once heard that doubting leads to asking questions and seeking answers, meaning that you care.

So, if I distrust God sometimes, it actually pushes me to seek Him and to draw nearer and learn more about Him than I ever have before. In a way, it can be a blessing, however, you do not want to stay in that place and live in doubt and fear. I will challenge you today to lay your fears of the world at the foot of the cross and to trust in God's will for your life. It may not be easy, and you may have to pray daily for the heart of surrender and trust, but it is completely worth it.

God actually wants us to come to Him at all times, but especially in moments of fear and anxiety. One of the verses that I hold dear to my heart is 1 Peter 5:7.

> Cast all your anxiety on him because he cares for you.

A relationship is a two-way street. God cares so very much for you and so in return, we should care enough to get to know Him better. Can you imagine being in a relationship where you only spend one hour a week with that person? Or maybe even only two times a year? How sad would that be? I know that God is saddened by many that treat Him this way, and/or practice religion over relationship, because He so desperately wants a personal relationship with each and every one of us! Revelation 3:20 is such a beautiful verse for depicting the kind of relationship that God wants with us. It says,

> Here I am! I stand at the door and knock. If anyone hears my voice and opens the door, I will come in and eat with that person, and they with me.

I make it a practice in my life to talk to God throughout my day, as if He is my friend and I am reminded of the hymn that my mom always sang to me of "What a Friend We Have in Jesus" because it is so true! How blessed are we to have that kind of personal connection to our savior? I know that I am humbled with a grateful heart to know that He loves me so much to save me from my sins and promise me eternity in heaven . . . because it could have stopped there.

BUT God.

He also provided us with the Bible, an entire instructional guidebook for how to live this life, a personal relationship with Him, our creator, and the Holy Spirit, who lives within us and also guides us throughout this life. I knew all this, and I should have been set, and yet I regretfully told God that I would do things my own way. So, on that one dreaded day in October of 2020, I made an impulsive decision that led to a long, hard journey ahead of me.

QUESTIONS TO THINK ABOUT

1. If you experience or have experienced distrust in the world, when did it start for you and how do you feel about it now?

2. Do you struggle with forgiveness? Who are the people in your life that you still need to forgive?

3. Do you or have you ever had distrust in God? What would it be like to honestly tell Him that and ask Him to help you trust Him?

4. What does your relationship with God look like right now? Is there anything that needs to change for you to grow closer to Him?

Chapter 3

Facing Reality

IT SEEMED LIKE AN ordinary day when I woke up that morning, aside from the exhaustion that was draining me. I wasn't sure that I could make it another day as I went through the motions of attending class and work. By the end of the day, I just did not feel like I could handle it anymore. I remember sitting in my car feeling completely numb and tired after trying to attend church worship practice, which had apparently been cancelled.

I should have been glad, and yet I felt nothing at all. I drove back to campus and on the drive back was when I told God that I just wanted to go home . . . not home on earth . . . but heaven. I remember parking near the dining hall and telling myself that I would have my last meal. I remember making it back to the dorms and telling myself to take my last shower. The rest is a blur, but I still see bits and pieces.

I remember overdosing on all my medications. I remember laying my head down to sleep and telling God that I would see Him soon, but that was the moment that regret slapped me right in the face. "What did I just do?" I asked myself as my life flashed before my eyes. I got glimpses of all the laughter of my friends in the last two years and the precious memories I made with countless people. And yet, it was already too late.

The next time I woke up, I was on the floor, shaking, tingling, and numb. I struggled to breathe and I knew that my heart was racing too fast. My vision was blurry. I think I was hallucinating a pool of sticky goo on the ground, and I could barely move. I wondered how I was possibly still alive because there was simply no way . . .

BUT God.

Somehow, my phone found its way into my hand, but it was shaking so bad that I kept dropping it. Somehow, I managed to dial my friend's number. Somehow, it just so happened to be the friend that was the RA on-call for the night. Somehow, she answered my call in the middle of the night, where I was told that I mumbled random things. Somehow, my door was unlocked. Somehow, the paramedics arrived on time. If that was not God, I don't know what else to believe. After all, the verse, Luke 1:37 tells us,

> For nothing will be impossible with God. (ESV)

He saved me for a reason, and my time in the hospital was a face-to-face look at reality. God did not stop there because He made me see and hear the possible consequences of my actions and makes me remember it to this day. As I fought for my life, in liver failure and with heart damage, I hallucinated some very raw, possible realities. It started with the cries, the wailing, and the mourning of all my loved ones as if they were in the hallway, right outside my hospital room. The moment I heard them, I started sobbing and the nurse ran in to ask me why I was crying.

"My loved ones are outside the door, but they won't come in to see me," I mumbled out in between stifled sobs.

She looked confused.

"There's no one out there," she said.

"Yes, I can hear them and see them walk past," I insisted, sobbing even harder.

We argued for a few minutes before she gave up and walked out. That's when I heard my mom's voice above all the others.

"Why did you do this?" she cried.

I cried back,

"I'm sorry . . . why won't you come in?"

"I can't," she answered.

"Why?" I cried.

"I need you."

She cried louder.

"I can't see you like this."

"Mommy . . . please," I begged as this conversation repeated itself over and over again.

The nurse came in a few more times to argue with me that there was no one outside my door until eventually, she grew tired of hearing my cries into the hallway. The next time she came in, she threw my cell phone at me that I was not supposed to have, and said,

"please just call someone."

I was confused, but I immediately dialed my mom, who asked me where I was.

"I don't know," I cried.

"What do you mean you don't know?" my mom had asked.

I later learned that she was worried that I had been kidnapped since it seemed as though no one knew where I was when she was looking for me. She lectured me about paying attention to my surroundings before I cut her off.

"But you know!" I said desperately.

"Know what?" she asked.

"Where I am . . . but you won't come in to see me," I sadly replied.

"What are you talking about?"

"You're in the hallway, right outside!" I cried.

"What, no . . ." she answered, but I think she sort of figured it out because she hung up with me not long after, either that or she realized that she would not get anything else from the conversation because I was clearly not in my right mind.

I continued to hear crying right outside my door when she hung up, but I was getting more glimpses of conversations. My loved ones were talking about me as if I had already died and they were planning my funeral.

"No, I'm not dead!" I cried.

"I'm still here . . . I'm right here!"

It was a living nightmare as my heart completely tore apart for the loved ones that cried over me . . . so close, and yet so far out of reach. I cried out to God,

"okay, I get it . . . please . . . I've had enough"

It was not until a day later that the voices subsided when I was transferred to another room . . . I guess God wanted to make sure that I really learned my lesson, but if that were the case, He should have let it go on for much longer . . .

As I was being transferred, I felt my world shatter when reality dawned on me that there really was nobody in the hallway outside my room. I was horrified with shame and embarrassment because I finally realized that it was all in my head.

"Oh my gosh, I'm so, so, so sorry," I told the staff around me.

They just gave me a few odd looks until we made it to my new room, where the new doctor and nurse arrived at the same time to introduce themselves. I wasn't really paying attention because I was still horrified about my hallucinations and the headache it must have caused the staff. That was until I heard the word Covid-19.

"What?" I asked.

"You're in the Covid unit now because you tested positive," the doctor said.

"I don't have Covid," I said.

"I can't have Covid."

The doctor and nurses gave each other a look.

"We did test more than once," he said, and that was that.

Before they left the room, I gave out more apologies for my embarrassing behavior and the doctor just gave a wave.

"We've seen worse," he said and walked out.

During my time on the Covid floor, God truly blessed me with some pretty amazing nurses and techs. For one, I still had my cell phone with me when I technically still wasn't supposed to have it as a psychiatric (psych) patient. God did that and sent me a nurse that would take it and charge it for me with their own personal charger.

God also sent me a nurse that would hang out with me anytime they had a break, because apparently, they said that they liked my company, so that was nice. God also sent some staff members that were believers who poured into me and encouraged me to continue living this life. However, I still became very anxious that I was not always told what was going on with me.

Anytime I talked to my mom on the phone, she and my dad were insistent that I leave the hospital when I could and return home with them. They remembered how mental illness was treated in the past and asked me if I really wanted to be locked up in an asylum for the rest of my life. It scared me and so I started to ask to leave even though my body was not completely healed yet.

BUT God.

He performed a miracle.

By the time I left the hospital Against Medical Advice (AMA), the doctor was a bit confused because both the liver failure and the heart damage reversed and healed itself. In fact, all abnormalities were gone . . . I had heard of miracles happening before, especially because my mom is a walking miracle as a polio survivor, however, I was not prepared to experience one myself. I was also confused, but grateful to still be alive and not have lasting consequences. I asked God if this was really happening, and I wonder today if any of you have ever experienced a miracle and felt similar feelings. In Job 5:9, it says,

> He performs wonders that cannot be fathomed, miracles
> that cannot be counted.

Perhaps God should have humbled me in that moment because the enemy slipped it into my mind that I had somehow conquered death . . . when in reality, God had saved me from dying and Jesus is the only one who defeated death forevermore when He rose from the dead. It says in Revelation 1:18,

> I am the Living One; I was dead, and now look, I am alive
> for ever and ever! And I hold the keys of death and Hades.

We must be careful of the lies that we are told because not only can they make us feel worse about ourselves, but they can also inflate our pride. If not careful, you may even start to believe that you do not need God, much like I thought I could survive on my own, however, we know how that turned out. I would soon find out that God would humble me many times over, especially after I felt pride about surviving a near-death experience. I know now to express gratitude for His patience and goodness any opportunity that I am given.

When I was told about my miracle, that is also when I was told that no psych hospital would take me because I was positive with Covid. I still had more days to quarantine, which actually worked in my favor because they let me leave to go home, even though I had to be shamefully escorted by the police, just so they could make sure that I would be safe.

However, it was a mistake to step back into my abusive home, quarantined, or not. Childhood memories seemed to flood me, even when I did not want them to. Internally I wanted to scream because everything in the house seemed to be a trigger as much as I tried to hold myself together. I was reminded of the yelling between my parents, specific moments when my father would demand my mother to leave, but she could not take me with her. Other times when volcanoes erupted over the smallest inconveniences.

I was reminded of the bulletin board outside the door to my room, which haunted my dreams because of the comparison placed in front of me and the reminders that I was never good enough. There was always someone that was better than me. There was always a need to strive for "perfection." And so not long after my quarantine ended, I moved back into the dorm hall to resume my RA duties.

I felt shame and embarrassment to walk back on campus after what I had put my friends, coworkers, bosses, professors, and residents through. It made it even harder for me when I was welcomed back with open arms and showed so much love and care. The friend that had saved me was my roommate during freshman year of college, but I felt like the recent events connected us on a level that no one would be able to understand.

Apparently, she had held me as we waited for the paramedics to arrive and as much as I desperately wish this experience was not a part of my story, I would not change what God had planned, because my friend would eventually accept Jesus into her heart because she prayed for me to live and without a doubt, God heard her prayers! This is the perfect example of God turning brokenness into a blessing and that He works all things for good as we are told in Romans 8:28.

> And we know that in all things God works for the good of those who love him, who have been called according to his purpose.

After my experience in the hospital and being back home to quarantine, I was faced with the reality that something in my life needed to change. I was still struggling with flashbacks and night-mares and extreme anxiety in public that sometimes led to panic attacks, which led me to find a therapist. Surprisingly, my mom had a change of heart after my suicide attempt and had started to seek therapy for herself.

Not only that, but she started to educate herself on mental illness, joining support groups and attending workshops or pre-sentations. It meant the world to me that she was trying to connect with me and to understand how she could support. By the time spring rolled around, therapy was simply not enough for me, and I started to seek more intensive help, however, I was still very clue-less about the mental health world.

BUT God.

Somehow, I reconnected with an old friend who opened up about her own struggles on social media. She was the first person I had ever known, to post on social media the words and pictures that showed real, raw, authentic truth to how she was doing in life. It was life-changing for me. I was inspired that she was brave enough to share her story and so I reached out to her. It was not long before she recommended a treatment program that she had gone through herself.

I was beyond thankful, and my heart was full when my mom was the one that drove me to my intake appointment. What I did not know at the time, was that this was about to start a treatment cycle that I was not necessarily prepared for . . . but then again, no one would ever be prepared on the journey to healing.

On the topic of facing reality, I was about to face the reality of the treatment world for mental health. It would be filled with so much brokenness that would break my heart too many times to count. It would leave me in tears, frozen with fear, uncertain about the future, continuing to doubt God. It would have me hear the stories of others, to connect in ways I never thought I could, to understand how God's heart breaks for us too. It would have me on my knees, shaking in corners, passed out on the floor. It would make me feel out of control, trapped, misunderstood, and all the more passionate about advocating for the mental health world.

I wonder what realities you have had to face in life or what realities lie ahead of you, patiently waiting for you to meet them face-to-face. I would encourage you to pray for what God will reveal to you in these moments. If you are not sure what to pray for or how to pray in preparation for facing realities, especially hard truths . . . I will encourage you with the verse in Romans 8:26–27.

> In the same way, the Spirit helps us in our weakness. We do not know what we ought to pray for, but the Spirit himself intercedes for us through wordless groans. And he who searches our hearts knows the mind of the Spirit, because the Spirit intercedes for God's people in accordance with the will of God.

This has always been a comfort to me as I am reminded that I do not always have to know what to pray for because the Holy Spirit lives within and knows our heart. The Spirit will intercede for us, but also, know that prayer does not need to be perfect. I speak to God as I would a friend, but still out of reverence and respect. I am certainly not going to start the conversation with "hey bro," or "dude."

He deserves much more respect than that, however, I do know that He knows our personality best and so if I am casually talking to Him, I don't necessarily feel pressure to try to be someone that I am not. I can have confidence that He hears me for me, knows every prayer sent His way and sees the desires of my heart. In Jeremiah 29, the prophet Jeremiah sends a letter to the exiles of what God wanted them to know, and in verses 12–13, they are told,

> Then you will call on me and come and pray to me, and I will listen to you. You will seek me and find me when you seek me with all your heart.

The same can be said for us today, as this was written in a time where Jesus had not yet come to take His place on the cross. If God tells the people of the Old Testament that He listens and will be with them, then how much more will He listen and be with us today when we have a direct relationship with Him? How much more will He hold our hand and guide us through this life? How much more will He bring us comfort and answer our prayers when the Holy Spirit lives within us? The extent of His love is overwhelming!

So, I don't know about you, but if I could tell 21-year-old me all these things, I may have had a different outlook on the realities I was about to face. With a God so great and the strength He gives, there is no reality that we shouldn't be able to face!

QUESTIONS TO THINK ABOUT

1. Have you had a "What did I just do?" moment in life before that was filled with regret? Are you able to forgive yourself for it?

2. Have you ever experienced a miracle or know someone who has? What were some of the feelings you encountered, and did you have a heart of gratitude or disbelief?

3. What are your initial thoughts about mental health treatment? Do past mistakes in society's treatment of mental illness influence how you view mental health treatment today?

4. What were the times that you had to face reality? Was it a wakeup call?

Chapter 4

Honesty Is Best

IT WAS A BLESSING from God that the treatment program I started in April of 2021 was a faith-based program, but it only lasted about three to four days and I will tell you why, while also reassuring you that I would be able to complete the program months later . . . just after a few detours . . .

It was a Partial Hospitalization Program (PHP), meaning that I spent about half the day in group therapy for five to six times a week. However, I was struggling so much at that point that I needed even more intensive care. A few days into treatment, my therapist held me back at the end of the day because I had refused to talk during the group. I did not want to tell her why . . .

BUT God.

I kept feeling that nudge that I needed to be honest, and I argued with Him internally that I was scared out of my mind. I tried to use other excuses. I tried to buy myself some time, but eventually, I spilled the truth. The truth was that I had planned to overdose again and had bought medications the night prior, but a friend knew that I was struggling and made me spend the night at her house so that I could not do anything before showing up for treatment the next day. She wanted me to be truthful and get the professional help, but I tried to fight it, until the phrase "honesty is the best policy" hopped into my head. It's as cheesy as it sounds, but also incredibly helpful during a serious situation.

I was immediately walked over and admitted to their in-patient, psychiatric hospital, my first ever experience of a psych ward. Not only that, but I was placed on the highest form of care for an entire week, meaning that I always had to have a staff member within arm's length of me . . . and yes, that even includes when you are in the bathroom or the shower. My privacy was completely taken from me. I will even go as far as telling you and embarrassing myself that I developed urinary retention and ended up in the Emergency Room (ER) because . . . well . . . could you go if you had someone staring at you?

This is the chapter where I tell you what it is like on the inside of a psych ward. Know that I do not share any of this to scare any-one or to make you feel sorry for me and those with mental illness. We are stronger than you think! Know that I am only sharing this to bring awareness, especially to those in the Christian world that do not hear a lot about this topic.

It was a major wake up call for me to see the brokenness of our world up close and personal. Of course I had heard stories from my father about prison life, stories I should have never been told, but to meet people for myself and to be struggling myself . . . that was a whole other world. It was indeed a culture shock for me as I grew up in the church and around many people who appeared to be rather put together . . . but in the psych ward . . . nobody seems to care what anyone thinks.

Tantrums were thrown on the floor. Fights would break out. Things would be tossed around. Someone even broke one of the only phones we could use (if you can imagine the riot that caused). Privileges were taken away. Food fights actually happened. Scream-ing, yelling, and profanity were the norm. People walked around in hospital gowns, grippy socks, house slippers, pajamas, tattered clothing, anything, you name it. I remembered feeling extremely uncomfortable my first day there . . . that was until a yelling match sent me into a flashback in the middle of the hallway. That was just perfect. Because from then on, everyone, including the doctors, thought that I was psychotic.

"I'm not crazy," I snapped.

"Well, it's just that you're seeing and hearing things that are not there," the doctor said.

"I told you. . .those things actually happened to me."

"Yes, but they're not happening now," he countered.

"Exactly. I told you . . . they're flashbacks," I said.

He was silent for a moment.

"But hallucinatory in nature?"

I shrugged.

"I'm not crazy," I said.

This conversation went on for much longer than it should have. It led to many more conversations about the type of care that I would need after leaving the hospital. My treatment team started to discuss long-term care facilities for me, and I was frozen with fear, thinking that my parents were right that I would be locked away for the rest of my life.

I tried my best to be overly complaint, but I still had nightmares most nights, and the fights and yelling would still send me into a flashback, no matter how hard I tried to fight it. I asked God, "why." I told Him that this couldn't be my life, and yet again . . . I felt that nudge to be honest with not only myself, but with the people around me.

I started to really try and get to know the people around me. I even opened up a little bit about my story during our therapy groups. To my surprise, I met people from many different walks of life. Veterans and people with families, children, fulfilling careers. I met someone that was a police officer and someone that was a neurosurgeon . . . a neurosurgeon!

If that tells you anything, it means that as a human, we are all broken and capable of hitting rock bottom moments or hitting a stumbling block in life. It means that any and everyone can struggle. It means that anyone can have an invisible disability. It means that anyone might hit a depressing point as I met some mothers with post-partum depression. It means that anyone might be hiding severe anxiety inside as I met another college student. I didn't feel so alone and abnormal anymore, although I know that God wishes that I did not feel this way at all.

If only it were so easy to fully rely on knowing that God is always with me and that He does not see me as crazy or abnormal. However, I know that I fall short . . . in fact, we all do as we are told in Romans 3:23.

> For all have sinned and fall short of the glory of God.

If you truly think about it . . . this world might as well be one big psychiatric hospital with God as our doctor and healer. He is, after all, the ultimate healer!

I know that I care too much about what other people think about me. That's one of the areas I fall short in and so perhaps that was why I was so concerned about this long-term care my treatment team kept bringing up. I finally told the other patients about this, and they tried to encourage me to go and get the help I needed. *Okay. . .that's not what I wanted to hear.* I remember thinking to myself.

BUT God.

Here we go again . . . He nudged me to be honest and to be more open to the conversation. I remember crying in my room, scared out of my mind about what this would mean for my life. I worried about what other people would think about me. I worried that people would treat me differently, if they did not already. I ultimately worried about being judged because my "perfect" façade had completely fallen away. BUT God reminded me that I should not be trying to please the world because He is the only one that is deserving to be pleased. First Thessalonians 2:4 says,

> But just as we have been approved by God to be entrusted with the gospel, so we speak, not to please man, but to please God who tests our hearts. (ESV)

I don't know about you, but I have to remind myself more often than not that I am not on this earth to please the people around me because my eyes should be fixed on the creator of the universe and the only one deserving to be pleased and praised. So, when I woke up the next morning and met with my treatment team, I honestly told them that I needed to work on the trauma and that if they wanted to send me somewhere, it should be somewhere that I can focus on healing. And so, the search and intake assessments for trauma residential treatment centers started.

I also wanted to mention that not all parts of the psych ward are scary like the things I listed off towards the beginning of this chapter. Although there are very many tears and loud expressions of emotion most of the time, there are also lots of meaningful conversations. The psych ward is a place to feel connected to others who understand you more than the outside world would. It is a place to help you find your voice and practice advocating for yourself. It is a place to stabilize you so that you can live your best life when you go back to your daily life.

Every hospital is different, and I will go into this more in the following chapters as I dive deeper into my story. However, for this hospital, it was faith-based and so I was blessed to have a worship service on Sundays and Bible study on Wednesdays. There were also many group therapies throughout the day ranging from art therapy, music therapy, recreation therapy, psychotherapy and educational groups that taught on mental wellness. It was truly a blessing because we would even get to play outside at times (basketball, volleyball, soccer, drawing with chalk) and there was a gym where we even had a ping pong table! I'm not saying that it was luxurious, but it was nice to still be treated just like a human.

During my entire time at the hospital, it did feel freeing to not have to cover up who I was. I was accepted for who I was, no questions asked. I mean, sometimes someone would lean over and ask, "what's your problem?" or "what are you in here for?" It was not out of malicious intent, but more out of curiosity and searching for ways to connect. When I think of my many hospital days where I did not feel the pressure of the world to conform to "perfection" and everyone else around me, it makes me think if that is how I am supposed to feel in general. Let me explain.

In the psych ward, you are not condemned for your struggles and your flaws. You are not condemned for your tantrums and breakdowns. You are not condemned for crying or screaming. You are not condemned for feeling the pain and heaviness of this world. You are not condemned for depression or anxiety or whatever it is they diagnose you with. You are not condemned for your story. In fact, you are supported and cared for. You are loved and encouraged. You are given hope. Is this not the perfect, beautiful example of what God does for us?

He supports, and cares, and loves, and encourages. He is our hope. He does not condemn you for your human struggles and flaws, the struggles of the flesh. However, I do not want this to become twisted into thinking that we will not face a judgement day in which we will escape being judged for our sins. This is not the case. The truth is that we should be judged because we are deserving of death as it says in Romans 6:23.

> For the wages of sin is death, but the gift of God is eternal life in Christ Jesus our Lord.

And there it is again. BUT God gave us the gift of salvation. He is merciful and gracious beyond anything I can possibly comprehend. Something that I have struggled with for a long time is trusting that this mercy and grace is truly real. It just seems too good to be true sometimes. I also struggle with thinking that I can have good things in life. So, a gift this big? How can it be? The only answer is love. Love beyond all comprehension. Perhaps the most famous verse in all the Bible is John 3:16.

> For God so loved the world that he gave his one and only Son, that whoever believes in him shall not perish but have eternal life.

How could He have loved the entire world enough to sacrifice His own son? Think about something that you have made with your own hands. Maybe it is a drawing, a painting, a special pasta dish, anything, but make sure that it was something that you were proud of. Now think about how you felt about your creation. Did you not love it? Well, God created this world. He created humans and He created each and every one of us.

So, there should be no question at all about whether or not He loved His creation because He deemed it good. In Genesis one, after every single day of forming the earth, God "saw that it was good." And yet we see that when God creates man, He uses the words "very good," so I can imagine that we are very much loved in every way.

Love is so incredibly powerful as God's love is what helped me throughout the long journey I am about to take you on. I have had some therapists even work with me to imagine God hugging me or feeling as though I was wrapped in His presence. For example, when I was crying in my closet as a child, I was told to imagine that Jesus walked in to let in the light and that He sat down on the floor next to me and held me. This kind of imagery could be very helpful for whatever situation you are in, if you are able to imagine Jesus embracing you or holding you in those difficult memories and/or moments.

However, because this chapter is about honesty, I will also say that being honest with myself, God, my treatment team, loved ones, and the people around me, is something that helped me along the way as well. If you can believe it, I actually used to be very closed off about my story. It is ONLY because of this treatment journey that God took me on, that I post on a blog monthly, occasionally with the National Alliance on Mental Illness, and it is why I can share my story with you today.

All the glory to God even through the hardships in my path of healing because as I mentioned before, He does turn ashes into beauty. I am a living testament to that through the many "BUT God" moments we have already had, and I haven't even told you my whole story yet.

I should explain how honesty is the best policy for me. Do you not want to be truly known by people and loved for who you are? This involves honesty. Do you not want to be regarded as trustworthy, responsible, and reliable? This involves honesty. Do you want healthy relationships and friendships? This involves honesty. If you take the time to really think about it, honesty is an important value to uphold. After all, the Ten Commandments given in Exodus twenty tells us just how important honesty is if God included the commandment,

> You shall not give false testimony against your neighbor.

If that doesn't convince you, the laws in Leviticus nineteen, given from God to Moses, to tell the Israelites, is much more direct. It says,

> Do not lie. Do not deceive one another.

Something that my father did teach me well during my childhood (although he really struggled to keep this value himself) was to always tell the truth. It has been ingrained into my mind if you will, and I am thankful for that. With that said, honesty helped me on my journey because it allowed my treatment team and support system to know how to best help me.

It allowed me to connect with people that I otherwise would have never even thought to talk to. It helped me to inspire and help others who were also struggling. It allowed me to heal to the point where I am living a joyful and fulfilling life right now, even through some of the struggles I still face.

Towards the end of my stay in the hospital, I was honest with my loved ones on the phone about what I needed their help to do. My mom and my friends would help to pack for me and buy my plane ticket to New Mexico where I would spend some time living at a residential treatment center that specialized in trauma.

I was also honest with my college professors about my struggles, hospitalization, and where I was headed next, meaning that I would not be able to complete the school semester or take my final exams. This was very difficult for me to acknowledge because it went against every ounce of my perfectionistic, people-pleasing mind. However, I swallowed my pride but still cried myself to sleep that night.

BUT God.

He blessed me once again.

I am completely honest when I tell you that every single one of my professors gave me a passing grade for the semester. They were all A's except for one B and one C. Truly a blessing from God that He did not have to do for me . . . but as I told you before . . . His love is overwhelming!

QUESTIONS TO THINK ABOUT

1. When have you most evidently seen the love of God? Through the creation of something you have made? Having a child? Because of a relationship? People around you showing you love and kindness?

2. Is honesty something that you struggle with? What do you think it would be like to ask God for an honest heart or to give you opportunities to practice honesty?

3. Has God ever given you a blessing that you did not think you deserved? How grateful was your heart?

Chapter 5

Desperation in Darkness

TRAUMATIC MEMORIES ARE SHROUDED in darkness, leading to desperation.

It was in May 2021 that I found myself in the deserts of New Mexico, walking up to a cabin-like building. I was already miserable, not just because of why I was there, but because the scenery was absolutely dreadful, and my physical environment tends to have a big impact on my mood. The ground was dry and cracked, not a blade of grass in sight. Sure, there were some trees, but they were crooked and definitely not that green. The only greenery around was all the cacti, which I already knew would be a bad idea because I tended to self-harm with what I could find. *Not the cactus needles.* I told myself. Now I was absolutely certain that I was making the wrong decision. *God, seriously?* I thought.

I was given a brief orientation, signed paperwork, and then taken on a tour of the facility, which was more like a camp if you ask me. I was introduced to more people than I could count. Apparently, there were about fifty patients in total, which meant that there were about three to four people per cabin, with a few exceptions. As you can imagine, I became one of the exceptions . . . and this is where I explain a bit more about trauma to you, specifically in how it affects me.

If you've ever heard of the book, *The Body Keeps the Score* by Bessel van der Kolk, it is incredibly true that trauma is stored in the body, not just mentally, but physically. This was true for me in the sense that I could not be touched unexpectedly, or I would go into a flashback, meaning that I drop to the floor and curl up into a ball and stay there until I feel somewhat safe enough to come out, which was never . . . and so people would have to intervene to calm me.

My body would be physically shaking as I relived my worst nightmares, unaware of my actual surroundings and the people around me. Not only was I triggered by touch, but by loud noises or voices, emergency vehicle lights and sirens, and a list of many others. This was the norm for me, but I was always careful about ensuring that I avoided as many triggers as I possibly could. However, this would soon be impossible in a treatment center for trauma.

They barely even gave me time to settle in before I was slapped head-on with trauma work. We had many group therapies throughout the day, met for individual therapy about three to four times a week, and were given a list of projects that were to be completed and shared in group therapy in a timely fashion.

I remember the first time that I sat in group therapy, someone was sharing their trauma timeline in excruciating detail (exactly what it sounds like . . . a timeline that you create of every single traumatic moment that you have had in your life, and yes, they wanted you to be detailed). I managed to run out of the room before the flashback hit me right outside in the middle of the gravel pathway that led to all the different cabins. *This was not happening.*

I don't remember what happened next, but I know that I ended up at the nurse's station somehow. My therapist was there, and she wanted to know all about my reactions to triggers and what usually helps me.

"I don't know," I shrugged.

"Well, what has helped in the past?" she asked.

"I told you. I don't know . . . I've never . . . I don't really . . . I don't talk about this stuff," I finally said, something along those lines of mumbling.

"I see. So, you've never worked on your trauma before?"

"Nope," I replied, shaking my head,

"and now I really don't want to."

I kind of shut down at that point because there was no way that I was going to trust a bunch of strangers with my story, vulnerabilities, and insecurities, especially when I was miles away from my loved ones. It made it even more difficult that we were not allowed to have our cell phones at all because they were a technology-free facility as much as they possibly could be. The only contact with the outside world that we had was a fifteen-minute computer time and fifteen-minute phone calls on a land line occasionally throughout the week on assigned days. I remember thinking, *are we not in the 21st century?*

It was hard enough that we had to work through our worst traumas on a daily basis, but then to be cut off from our loved ones . . . I think that is what made me spiral the worst, other than the fact that I was being spiritually drained. I needed God so desperately and yet no one around me was a believer. I never got to see a single sermon because of the lack of technology. I started to forget about my Bible, and ultimately, I felt myself drifting further away from Him. *Was this a test of my faith?* In fact, the entire facility turned out to be a holistic healing community, meaning that they were influenced by the spiritual realm, if you will.

Acupuncture and Reiki were alternative treatments that were offered, but I declined in a heartbeat. I experienced my first sound bath, and it made me so uncomfortable that I ended up running out of the room. If you can guess, I ran out of group sessions A LOT. Yoga was also provided. We were taught about many superstitions that the Native Americans in the area believed, about herbs while we took care of a garden, and about burning incenses.

We also learned about essential oils, where I found that lavender is especially helpful in grounding me and keeping me present. Ultimately, if this were a test of my faith, I failed drastically . . . because in a place like this, it is way too easy to forget God and all the things He has done for you.

I still feel conviction today that I forgot Him at one of my weakest moments, because He should have been the very thing that I clung to. In Deuteronomy 6:12, Moses tells the Israelites,

> Be careful that you do not forget the LORD, who brought you out of Egypt, out of the land of slavery."

Much like the Israelites were brought out of slavery, I too, was brought out of the slavery of my sin when Jesus took His place on the cross and I believed in Him as my salvation. But not only that, because God had saved me from physical death several times already, I should have been on my knees in praise and thanksgiving. And yet there I was forgetting about the miracles in my life and trying to do things on my own, once again.

However, although I know God wants us to be aware of conviction and to turn back to Him, I also know that He does not want us to beat ourselves up about the sins of our flesh and our humanity. Just like God forgives us and we forgive others, we must also be forgiving of ourselves. I still struggle with this today because of the number of regrets that I hold, however, I am comforted by the verse, Philippians 1:6, that says that God will complete the "good work" that He began in us.

> And I am sure of this, that he who began a good work in you will bring it to completion at the day of Jesus Christ. (ESV)

I can be encouraged that because I am a child of God, He has begun a "good work" in me and although I will still sin and struggle on this earth, I have hope within my brokenness that I will be completed in Christ. This world and my struggles are only temporary as it says in 2 Corinthians 4:18.

> So we fix our eyes not on what is seen, but on what is unseen, since what is seen is temporary, but what is unseen is eternal.

Therefore, I want to encourage you that although I am about to share with you my desperation through darkness, at the end of the day, this was a testing of my faith. It was a lesson to be learned that I do have to rely solely upon God and that I do have a heavenly father that I can run back to, even if I've forgotten Him in a season of my life. After all, His work continues as He grows us through trials and tribulation as we are told in James 1:2–4.

> Consider it pure joy, my brothers and sisters, whenever you face trials of many kinds, because you know that the testing of your faith produces perseverance. Let perseverance finish its work so that you may be mature and complete, not lacking anything.

Equine and animal therapy were also therapeutic opportunities at the facility, and that, I was thankful for. My first time at equine therapy I was still shy around my peers and so I stayed near the fence. The horse we were working with was following commands from the therapist, but then he stopped when he saw me. I wonder if you've ever had that feeling that animals can just understand you on a level that humans cannot.

Tears started to fill my eyes because that horse came to me. I think he knew that I needed him and so as I hugged him, the therapist told me to feel his heartbeat because apparently horses can match your heartbeat and regulate it to help calm you. It's comforting and breathtaking, and this is where I thank God for His beautiful creation. I'm thankful that He gave us animals to care for and that they can also provide some comfort for us.

Another very popular type of therapy at this treatment center was art therapy. They were ALL about the art. I think I did more art projects than I did in all my years of childhood combined. Okay, that might be a bit of a stretch, but we did a lot. The most popular pastime was to paint "anger rocks" in which we would paint rocks with negative emotions, painful memories, reminders, or anything that we wanted to let go of, and then we would toss the rocks over a fence and cliff at the edge of the property. The art room was one of my favorite places to be, other than being outside, because besides that, there wasn't much else we could do.

In terms of individual therapy, I had the typical psychotherapy, but I also had EMDR, which stands for Eye Movement Desensitization and Reprocessing where you literally move your eyes or tap your hands while recounting traumatic events in detail and also doing the same for a safe place that you create in your mind. My safe place was a small teal house in the jungles of Malaysia (where my mom's family is from) and there were butterflies everywhere and a stream ran next to the house, visible through the trees.

I also had somatic therapy which focused more on the mind-body connection. I did not really like my sessions because they felt like too much for me. For example, my therapist would have me hold a bundle of blankets as if I were holding my inner child, or she would have me push her away in a rolling chair when yelling "no," and well, I don't yell and I struggled to feel like I had a voice for myself, so that didn't work.

This is where desperation started to settle in. The more I tried to battle the darkness within, the more desperate I became, and I did not know how to properly cope without turning to maladaptive behaviors. I started to harm myself by scratching or by picking cactus needles. Nightmares plagued me every single night to the point where I had to be heavily medicated just to sleep. Flashbacks were then happening multiple times a day and the staff were getting desperate too. At one point, I was on more than ten psychiatric medications.

As I told you in the beginning, I became an exception because I was moved into a tiny room in the nurse's station that felt more like a closet. They wanted to always have eyes on me, but I was also placed on fifteen-minute checks so that they could keep track of how I was doing from one moment to the next. Just between you and me, it got really annoying to be asked how I was doing or if I needed anything every fifteen minutes, but I understand why they did it.

If you didn't already think that things were going downhill, I completed my trauma timeline and was told to share it in group. *You're joking, right?* I remember thinking to myself. *This is going to be a disaster.* And I was not wrong. Suicidality hit me the instant I began sharing, and when I was done, I wanted nothing more than to disappear from the world or to hurt myself so badly that the physical pain could overtake the pain I felt inside (this is what it is like for someone that self-harms because I know that this is a very difficult thing for most people to understand unless you struggle with it yourself). Apparently, I was honest about this during the flashback I was having and so an ambulance came to take me away. That would be the first out of four times I went to the ER for overnight observation during my time in New Mexico.

Towards the end of my time there, the darkness of desperation overpowered me, and I did not end up completing the program because things continued to escalate when I attempted suicide for the second time. I was still on fifteen-minute checks and yet I somehow managed to be missing for over two hours.

BUT God.

He saved me yet again.

My friend found me nearly unconscious due to blood loss and ran to get the nurses. I don't remember anything else except for waking up in the hospital and being told that I would be transferred to my second psychiatric inpatient hospital when I was medically stable. That inpatient stay was more traumatic than my first. The beds were made of plastic, with only a thin sheet to cover it, meaning the hard surface was quite uncomfortable and I was freezing most of the time.

It was my first morning in the common area, sitting in a plastic chair and watching "The Big Bang Theory" for the hundredth time because that's one of the only things they let you watch in a psych ward. It was either that or some random game show because we could not watch the news or anything romance, action, or thriller/horror related in case it would trigger or set someone off. Why we still did not have other options . . . I don't know. Anyway, I was sitting there, minding my own business when the breakfast trays were being handed out and I was hit smack dab in the face with a cup of orange juice just as yelling and fighting broke out. I froze, disassociated, and went into a flashback.

When I finally came back to my senses, I was in my bed where I had apparently fallen asleep. The nurse came in a few moments later to check on me and she told me what had happened. Apparently, as the techs were breaking up the fight, this nurse had been trying to get me out of the way. She said that she had to guide me to my room where I sat in the shower, hospital gown and all. It was her that had helped dry me off, gave me a new gown, and got me into bed. I think my face turned red because I was completely filled with shame and embarrassment, and I kept apologizing to her.

"What are you apologizing for? Being mentally ill?" she asked.

"You didn't have to do that," I told her, shaking my head.

"It's not your fault," she said, and I never knew just how much I needed to hear those words.

She was the source of encouragement that God placed for me during my time there. The days blurred together with playing basketball in the gym or coloring in art, but aside from that there wasn't much to do except watch mindless TV, puzzle in the corner, or read one of the only five books they had. I didn't even have my Bible with me . . . in fact, I had none of my belongings. However, I was soon released and taken back to my residential facility where I learned that not long after, my mom and her friend would be flying out to get me. *Thank goodness.* I wanted to get out of there as soon as possible.

A few days before I was to leave, I was called to the office to talk to the CEO of the facility. He told me that my friend's mom was suing and that she, along with a few of the other patients were leaving that day because they felt as though my actions were traumatic for them and that the facility did not handle my case as they should have.

He wanted to hear my own thoughts and, in that moment, when I should have spoken up and told him what could have been done differently or how they could improve, I regretfully shrugged it off. I think that I was too exhausted to talk and advocate for myself, especially because I was only allowed to leave because my mom was coming to get me, but the deal was that I had to be taken back to the same inpatient psych hospital that I started at.

The day my mom and her friend arrived to pick me up, my arm was still heavily wrapped, and I know it broke my mom's heart. When she hugged me, I never wanted to let go. I wanted to apologize over and over again. I wanted to promise that I would be okay . . . and yet the journey was far from over. The desperation in darkness was far from gone as I continue to share my story with you.

BUT God.

I write to you today to give you a glimpse into the present reality that I am living in. That desperation no longer lives inside of me. The darkness is still there in pieces, but God is slowly chipping away and healing those wounded areas. I would like to share some verses with you about God's light in the darkness.

> The light shines in the darkness, and the darkness can never extinguish it. (John 1:5 [NLT])

> This is the message we have heard from him and declare to you: God is light; in him there is no darkness at all. (1 John 1:5 [NLT])

> For you were once darkness, but now you are light in the Lord. Live as children of light. (Ephesians 5:8)

> He has delivered us from the domain of darkness and transferred us to the kingdom of his beloved Son. (Colossians 1:13 [ESV])

> When Jesus spoke again to the people, he said, "I am the light of the world. Whoever follows me will never walk in darkness, but will have the light of life." (John 8:12)

So, sweet friends . . . be encouraged by these verses in knowing that light will always shine through the darkness, that God is light and no darkness exists within Him, that we are made to be children of light (remember the children's song, "This Little Light of Mine," if not, I encourage you to go listen to it again), that we have been delivered from the darkness, and that we are blessed to have the light of life.

QUESTIONS TO THINK ABOUT

1. How has desperation played a part in your life? It may not look like my story but think about impulsive decisions you have made or desperate longing that has otherwise led you to do something you would not normally do.

2. If you have experienced trauma, how do you think your body has internalized it? And how does it manifest when you are reminded of the traumatic memory? Have you ever thought of working through your trauma to give yourself the chance of complete healing?

3. What trials and tribulation are or have been the testing of your faith? Are you willing to allow yourself to learn and grow from them?

4. Are you allowing God's light to shine through you? Will you allow Him to chip away and heal the darkness inside of you?

Chapter 6

Breaking Trust

I WAS WOKEN UP to more explosive yelling, right back at the same psych hospital I started at. *Not Again.* I meant that both literally about the yelling and about being at the same place I started. The staff still remembered me, and I know they gave me that look of, *oh, you're back already.*

"It didn't work, okay?" I remember telling one of the nurses.

"What didn't?" she asked.

I rolled my eyes and sighed. It was no use explaining myself over and over again. Obviously, I meant the treatment center for trauma they sent me to. I know that they knew it too because the doctors were desperately trying to get me off a lot of the medications that I got put on while trying to work on my trauma. For one, I was on way too many sleeping medications to the point where when I got up in the middle of the night to go to the bathroom, I passed out right on the floor. They fixed that quickly. Another medicine was making my vital signs unstable, either that or it was the undetected Anorexia at this point. I kept that well-hidden . . .

Anyway, when they were finally happy with the way my medications looked, they started to talk about my discharge plan. However, I told them that I didn't have much of a choice except to go back home and they were very much against that.

"Didn't you say your household was abusive?" the doctor asked.

"Well, yeah, but what else am I supposed to do? I can't live at the college dorms anymore," I said.

The doctor was shaking his head.

"Not happening," he said, and got up to leave.

I was completely confused because the conversation couldn't be over. I later found out that he wanted to talk to my mom. Apparently, the hospital told my mom that they would not release me if I was going home and that an alternative option would have to be found. I'm not exactly sure how the conversation went or who she talked to, but what I do know is that they gave her a hard reality to face and told her that she needed to decide between her husband, or her child. I can't imagine how she must have felt to be torn between two worlds and to always be the middle person.

When my mom and I mended our relationship months prior, she became my role model because she exemplifies Christ so well. Her ability to forgive and love my dad for who he is, has to be such a beautiful example of how Christ loves the church.

Although she separated from him in order to take care of me, and they are divorced today in protection of her own well-being and health, she tells me that she prays for him and hopes that people will come into his life that will be able to help and shepherd him. She is the reason why I was able to forgive him as well and still love him from afar. She does not talk bad about him or condemn him . . . instead, she reminds me of the good things that he taught me growing up and about his own brokenness that we pray God will heal. In Psalm 147:3, it says,

> He heals the brokenhearted and binds up their wounds.
> (ESV)

It is a blessing to know that God heals the broken and the wounded, however, we must remember that we must also be accepting of His healing. Those that do not know Him may not know of His healing because they have not yet grasped the extent of His power and love.

Therefore, God used my mom to save me from the system where I might have been lost. She took responsibility for my well-being, promising the hospital that she would not leave my side until I was healthy enough to gain independence. With that said, they discharged me into her care, and I stepped down to try their faith-based PHP program once again.

From the very beginning, my mom gave me routine, structure, and accountability as we settled into one of many hotels that we would live in over the summer of 2021. I went to treatment each day, reminding me of my grade school days and I would spend the evening playing music or watching movies with my mom. It was a time of rest and healing.

We had deep conversations, and she took care of my self-harm wounds so lovingly that they healed better than I could have ever asked for. This was another example of God's love. She treated my wounds and prayed over my scars and over my mind as I went to sleep each night. I would imagine that God would do the same. He cares for me in every way possible and He blessed me with a mother that would show me His love that compares to no other.

I was also shown His love in treatment each day as we read from His word and learned about what the Bible had to say in terms of mental illness. It was eye-opening to realize just how broken each and every person was in the Bible and how God still used many of these broken people to carry out His plans and promises. I realized that it could be me that He might use one day. I also connected well with the other patients, and we were able to be a source of support and encouragement for one another, reminded by the verse in 1 Thessalonians 5:11.

> So encourage each other and build each other up, just as you are already doing. (NLT)

My prayer for you today is that you have a group of believers around you that encourage and lift you up. I pray that you have a church community and are being fed spiritually. I pray that loved ones are supportive of you and that you have friends that you can laugh with and share secrets too. I pray that you have a support system that loves you for you and can be there for you in times of need, whether to be a listening ear or to physically step in to meet your needs. I pray that you are able to trust these individuals and the role they play in your lives, because although trust takes time to build, it is incredibly worth it to have people by your side that know you and your story to help you live a fulfilling life.

I was slowly building trust with my mom, loved ones, and treatment team. I completed the PHP program rather quickly and stepped down to the Intensive Outpatient Program (IOP) which meant I only had to go to treatment three times a week instead of five to six. My mom and I started talking about what the next step for me would be because I wanted to go back to college, however, I could not live on campus, and it was not wise for me to live on my own so soon. We were struggling to find options and it got to the point where I almost wanted to give up.

BUT God.

Somehow one of my mom's friends knew of a single Christian mom and her three kids that rented out two of their bedrooms to college students. They just so happened to be looking for someone to fill one of the bedrooms for the fall 2021 semester. Once pictures of the room were sent to me, I knew that I wanted to live there, especially when I found out that I knew two of the kids because they were close in age to me, and we used to be in church youth choir together. After more conversations about whether this was the right step for me, my mom helped me to pay the deposit, and I started searching for a part-time job.

By August 2021, I was living independently, but still looked out for by a family, and I had secured a job as a Mental Health Technician (MHT) for a local residential drug rehabilitation center. However, I should have known that I was not yet ready for a job like this because I was not completely healed myself. Although thankfully I do not struggle with drug or alcohol addiction, I have met people along my journey that do, and it is heartbreaking. A lot of them come from backgrounds of abuse and horrific traumas. A lot of them come from broken homes and have not been shown true love. A lot of them are just as broken as the rest of us.

In the beginning, I was not taken seriously in my job position because the patients thought that I was too "put together." That was, until I wore a short sleeve shirt for the first time and one of the patients saw my scars. The news seemed to spread like wildfire and suddenly I became the staff member that everyone wanted to talk to.

I became the person that they came to for advice. I became someone that could understand them on a level that other staff members could not. It was shocking to me because I never would have thought that when people knew about my brokenness, it could draw them closer to me. In my past experience, my own church and some people that I thought were friends, actually turned away and rejected me.

The rejection that hurt the most was when the church I grew up in gossiped about me until I could no longer show my face. The embarrassment and shame were too much to bear. I was judged for my struggles and not given the help that I asked for when I did. However, I do not hold it against them even though it still saddens me to think about . . . but what saddens me the most is not the rejection . . . it is the fact that the church should be an example of the love of Christ, loving and caring for everyone because church is the place for the brokenhearted.

It saddens me that someone may have walked through those doors and not felt heard or loved and then left without getting to know the love of Jesus. It saddens me that others may not be getting the help and spiritual food that they need. It saddens me that others may be rejected or judged and that they may lose faith in the God we trust. This would become a broken trust simply because we failed to do our part as the church. In 1 Corinthians 12, unity in the body of Christ is written about where there are many parts that make up the whole body (the church) under the authority of Christ. First Corinthians 12:12 says,

> Just as a body, though one, has many parts, but all its many parts form one body, so it is with Christ.

We are one body even though we are separate parts. There-fore, one part of the body cannot say that they do not need the other because as it says in 1 Corinthians 12:24b-26,

> But God has put the body together, giving greater honor to the parts that lacked it, so that there should be no divi-sion in the body, but that its parts should have equal con-cern for each other. If one part suffers, every part suffers with it; if one part is honored, every part rejoices with it.

Is it not true that the entire body of Christ suffers when just one part is injured? Think of the brokenness in this world. It is evident on every street corner. Should we not offer as much love as we can possibly give? If only we could offer as much support and encouragement to every part of the body as we wait here on this earth to be reunited with our king in heaven. Maybe at least then the world could be a bit more tolerable to live in . . . maybe . . .

So, as I settled into a new semester of college, a new job, and a new living situation, I kept up with seeing a trauma therapist and psychiatrist. I thought that I was doing well, however, I did not notice that I was relapsing in terms of Anorexia until it was much too late (it was always in the back of my mind as I struggled on and off throughout the years since the age of 12, however, many other things seemed to take precedence over treatment of this disorder).

It started with the excuse that I did not like to cook or spend my time in the kitchen since I never had before. I was obsessed with label reading and I kept a tight reign on my caloric intake. I went to an early morning swim practice on some days, running on other days, and did an obsessive number of workouts in my room.

I thought that I was just keeping myself healthy, but what I was really doing was suppressing trauma and negative emotions again to try and cope with life stressors. As you can imagine, it did not end up working. Everything spiraled downhill rather quickly when I wanted more feelings of control and so my food intake was restricted to the point where I did not eat for a week. And the worst part was that I wanted to keep starving and I did not want anyone to find out about it.

BUT God.

He did not let me stay hidden in my darkness.

At the time, I was doing EMDR with my trauma therapist and I was getting frustrated because it did not feel like we were making any progress. I walked into her office one afternoon, already annoyed when she did what she always did . . . she asked if I wanted a snack.

"Never," I said automatically without even realizing it.

She looked at me.

"Do you have an eating disorder that I don't know about? Is that why you always reject my snacks?"

I felt as though all the air in the room was sucked out.

"Well. . ." I froze.

"It's just never come up," I finished.

And my secret was out. And I was not happy about it.

I went home after that session feeling completely defeated and angry at both my therapist and God. I felt as though the one thing I controlled really well was being taken from me. Restricting my food intake gave me not only a sense of control, but it helped me to suppress and numb my emotions when I felt the hunger pains.

It helped to distract me from having to deal with and work through my trauma. It helped to get me praise, attention, and adoration. It helped to get me through many difficult years of my life and there was no way that I was letting anyone take that from me. And yet, I reluctantly contacted a dietician that specialized in eating disorders, and I scheduled an appointment with my Primary Care Physician (PCP).

Here came the worst news . . . my treatment team wanted to send me back to treatment, meaning to live at another residential treatment facility. I panicked. *There is no way. I just got my life back.* I remember thinking. I spiraled even further, started to abuse the diet pills I used, and relapsed on self-harming because the feelings were too overwhelming for restriction alone. And then, due to a weakened immune system and also because this was still during the time of the pandemic . . . I fell incredibly sick.

My mom stopped by to drop off food and medication when I fainted because I could barely walk, and I struggled to breathe. She ended up taking me to the hospital where I was told that I had Covid pneumonia in both of my lungs, and not only that . . . I had refeeding syndrome (a life-threatening condition caused by re-introducing food after a long period of starvation or malnutrition) because I had tried to eat again after going another week without food.

Again, the topic of treatment came up and so I reluctantly got placed on a waitlist for a teenage/young adult ED (eating disorder) residential treatment center in the south part of Texas. It was not an ideal situation to wait, however, I had to go back to my PCP to complete medical paperwork for the treatment facility and my situation only got worse.

When I got to the doctor's office, I was shaking, sweating, and panicking because I knew that I had taken too many diet pills that morning. I didn't mean to, but I was already freaked out that they were going to have me step on the scale, and I felt like I had to try to do something to influence the number, even though realistically, diet pills don't work like that. Well, I didn't know that at the time.

The doctor immediately sensed that something was wrong, and they performed an Electrocardiogram (EKG) because it was also needed for my medical paperwork. When he walked back into the room, I pretty much read his face when he told me that he called an ambulance.

"What?" I asked, as if I didn't hear him the first time.

"It's just that your heartrate is really high, and your EKG is abnormal"

"I know, I can feel it," I said.

"Right," he said

"And you didn't think anything was wrong?" he asked.

I froze, never liking it when I get asked something where I have to be honest about my actions.

"It's because I took diet pills," I finally blurted out.

"Ah," the doctor said, starting the uncomfortable conversation where I had to spill the truth about the extent of my eating disorder.

That wasn't the only secret that I was caught in, because when the paramedics arrived, my doctor also saw my fresh self-harm wounds and he was afraid that they were infected because they should have been stitched up, but it was too late for that. He told me that he was going to have to tell my psychiatrist about it and that I should go to the hospital to be stabilized, and I panicked because at this point, my mom did not know about any of this. I had just gained her trust back and I did not want to break it all over again.

"No," I said.

"I'm fine, I don't have to go to the hospital"

"That's not what we're recommending," the doctor said.

"I just want to go home," I said, continuing to insist until I got my way.

I ended up having to sign that I was refusing treatment, and I left to run back to more maladaptive behaviors back at home since my emotions were on overload. It was not long before the dreaded appointment with my psychiatrist rolled around, and she made me show her my wounds. I also saw the look of concern on her face when she said that she had to call my mom, who held me as I cried and as I apologized to her many times over. I had to drop out of college and my mom was told to take me to the nearest psych hospital, however, when we got to the facility, they said that they were not medically equipped to care for me due to the ED.

I am so thankful for my mom that even though she was disappointed that I broke her trust in letting me live independently, she knew that I was close on the waitlist for the ED facility and instead of taking me to another hospital, she went ahead and drove me down to south Texas where we stayed with a friend until the spot opened up for me. God was still looking out for me, and He very much gave my mom discernment and wisdom in how to help and comfort me.

Throughout the time that I was living apart from my mom, I was actively trying to seek God desperately, however, there felt like a wall between me and Him, possibly because I was still hiding the ED, and I did not want to let Him fully in to heal that part of me.

In a way, without even realizing it, I was pushing Him away. I was choosing not to trust Him. I was breaking my own trust in myself and in Him.

This is not what He desires for us. He wants our trust and He wants us to depend on Him fully because He does know what is best for us, it just may not always be what we want in the moment. Proverbs 3:5–6 is a popular verse that says,

> Trust in the Lord with all your heart and lean not on your own understanding; in all your ways submit to him, and he will make your paths straight.

If only I would have been able to see it back then, that God's way would have been better. However, because I trusted in my "own understanding" and in my own maladaptive ways of coping, I most likely prolonged my suffering and learned things the hard way. Nonetheless, God still loved me in my brokenness, and He was patient as I learned to put my trust in Him again.

QUESTIONS TO THINK ABOUT

1. How do you best exemplify Christ? How might you improve in striving to become Christ-like? What are some steps you can take?

2. Are you accepting of God's healing or are you still holding onto something in "secret"?

3. Has anyone broken your trust now or in the past and how did it make you feel? Was the relationship mended or how did you move forward?

4. Have you ever broken anyone's trust? How did that make you feel, and did you do anything to try and gain the person's trust again?

Chapter 7

Defiant Fear

IF I COULD CHANGE anything in my past, it would be the story I am about to tell you in this chapter. And if you're wondering why . . . it is because I carry the most regret and shame for my defiant behavior throughout my time at my first ED residential treatment center. I did not act out because I wanted to cause harm or to make the staff work even harder or to bring attention to myself.

I acted out because of the amount of fear within me and because I did not know how to properly express the turmoil of emotions inside, meaning it was the first time that I was told I might have Borderline Personality Disorder (BPD), and the fear of that merely intensified my behavior because of the amount of stigma I had heard about the diagnosis. It did not help that this would be my longest stay at a treatment facility as I was there for almost five months, even spending Halloween, Thanksgiving, Christmas, and New Year's there.

It was bad enough that I was being forced to go. I was already mentally prepared to fight the system, making a very detailed plan about how I was to sneak diet pills and razors in. As much as I wish that it wasn't, my plan was successful. I was straight up in denial that Anorexia was a problem that needed to be addressed.

"It's not that bad," I remember telling the doctor and nurse that were doing my medical assessment.

"Right . . . your body is telling us otherwise," the doctor said.

Just to sum it up for you . . . my labs were all over the place, my heart rate and blood pressure were too low, my fingernails were purplish-blue due to poor circulation and I was just always cold. Not to mention the hair loss, fatigue, dizziness, nausea, and many other unpleasant symptoms. And yet, I stayed in denial for over half the time I was there.

The days were so much so the same that they all seemed to blur together. Our meals were at the same time every day to give us routine, but also to allow our bodies to adjust to eating consistently and in a timely manner. In between meals and snacks there were therapy groups, cooking exposures, and school time because everyone was either still in high school, or they were enrolled in college . . . everyone, except for me (I dropped out, remember . . . also very shameful for me). About once or twice a week we would have yoga and about once a month a therapy dog would come to visit.

Other than that, there wasn't much to do except personal art projects, playing the piano that they had, reading, or sitting outside in the grass. We also saw a dietician twice a week, a therapist three times a week, and a psychiatrist and doctor once a week. We also had blood drawn every week and some people would be allowed to go for a group walk occasionally.

Something that I did appreciate was the fact that we did get access to our cell phones every evening once we made it to a certain level in the program. I will save you the details, but basically if you did what you were supposed to and completed the therapy assignments that were given to you, then there were privileges that you could earn.

I was good at completing therapy assignments, even finding creative ways to complete them by collaging, drawing, or writing a song as I brought my guitar with me to the facility. I had my own collaging corner and there came a point where I made so many that the patients (only eight of us were treated at a time, so it was a very close-knit community) hung them all in our living room area (we lived in a huge house, almost like a mansion, which was nice because it made us at least feel more comfortable and not trapped or confined).

However, I struggled the most at being compliant with my meal plan. It was also a major culture shock for me because I was used to eating a primarily Asian diet and so I did not know many of the things that were served to us and how they were cooked. I didn't even know what a panini press was!

It was a very rough start for me in the beginning because I was having nightmares every night and so the staff woke me up sometimes to have me sleep on the couch. I would have flashbacks at least once a day, and I was also placed on a one-on-one observation level due to my suicidality and self-harm risk, meaning that I had to have a staff member always sitting next to me.

This lasted for about a week, however, as soon as they took me off, my first act of defiance was to overdose on the diet pills I had sneaked into the facility. I ended up fainting and I was taken to the hospital. You could say that I was very far from God at this point because I harmed myself out of anger towards Him. I told Him that I did not want to be in treatment and that I did not need to give Him the ED.

If you are wondering why, I did not know at the time, but I very much idolized the "thin ideal" because it matched my idea of perfectionism. I also had this false belief that as long as I held onto the ED, I could suppress the traumatic memories and negative emotions inside . . . I could numb the pain and pretend like everything was fine. In James 1:14, it says,

> But each person is tempted when he is lured and enticed
> by his own desire. (ESV)

My desire was focused so much on controlling my body and emotions that I was placing those desires above God Himself. Therefore, because I was in a treatment environment that was challenging those thoughts and beliefs about myself and my need for control, I pushed back immensely because I was not ready to let go . . . or if I am really honest . . . I did not want to let go.

I would hardly eat anything at all, and I continued to decline both mentally and physically. There came a point where the facility would call my mom to ask for help in how to encourage me to eat, but she was at a loss too because she was always too tired to fight with me about food . . . she had been fighting me my entire life.

You could say that the disordered eating started for me when I was a toddler . . . I would only eat peas and drink milkshakes. Whenever my mom took me to the doctor, they shrugged off her worries and said,

"she will eat when she is hungry."

"But she doesn't," my mom would argue, and yet the doctors never seemed to worry.

Throughout my childhood, I was an extremely picky eater, and many foods would give me severe anxiety, making me develop some interesting food rituals/habits. I am not exaggerating when I say that every meal was a fight in our house, and I never wanted to finish my plate and there would always be some odd reason. My dad would get so frustrated sometimes that he would make me sleep at the dinner table . . . therefore food became even more traumatic.

However, twelve years old was when I felt insecure about my body image and took control of my eating habits for myself as a coping mechanism, restricting my food intake and relying on protein drinks and supplements. I was a competitive swimmer, and this made a drastic spiral in my physical health. My middle school counselor told my parents that I needed treatment for Anorexia, but mental health was simply not a topic that was welcomed in our household, and so I suffered in silence. By the time I was fifteen years old, I had to give up swimming for many different reasons, but also because I wasn't sure if I could physically handle it anymore.

I continued to suffer in silence, on and off, until I ended up at this treatment facility at the age of 21. Walking into it was a very new world for me which is also why I was so fearful of the process. I had no idea what to expect. I was fearful of new surroundings, strangers, food, weight gain, traumatic reminders, and so much more, and then you toss in fear of the unknown? It was pretty much too much to bear. And this fear manifested itself in defiance.

I refused to listen to what the staff told me to do or when they encouraged me to eat. Sometimes I would even refuse to participate in certain groups. I self-harmed with whatever and whenever I could find something sharp. They had to take away far too many random things because I was too creative for my own good. I would sometimes throw away my medications so that I would not have to take them. I even punched a wall because I felt the urge to hurt myself and didn't have a means to do so.

This is not a picture of me that I wanted to paint for you. The people-pleasing in me screamed the whole time I've been writing this chapter, and yet I will shamefully admit that I would be robbing you of the whole picture if I did not include this part of my story. God laid it on my heart to include it because it shows you the extent of my brokenness. It shows you the drastic measures of my heart. There was a void inside me that I was trying to fill on my own, and nothing was working, leaving me even more frustrated and left in a cycle that I would be incapable of escaping if I did not let go of the very thing eating me up inside.

As I was faced with more probing questions to challenge the ED, major emotional dysregulation and PTSD intensified. I was soon on multiple medications again to help me sleep at night, but I still had disturbing nightmares sometimes. We were trying to monitor what would work best to prevent a flashback, but it seemed hopeless at the time. Some of the flashbacks got so bad that I accidentally dropped and shattered a plate one time, sending me crying and panicking, to locking myself in the bathroom because I thought it was my closet, and the staff panicked because it took them almost an hour to find me.

So, as my mental health continued to cause issues, my physical health followed suit. I fainted while walking down the stairs one morning and another time during yoga. I was blessed that I was not severely injured, however, the dizziness was getting worse, where my vision would go black every single time I stood up. In fact, all the unpleasant symptoms were getting worse, and yet I still refused to even eat half of my meal plan.

The doctor would point out that I had orthostatic hypotension (your blood pressure drops with position changes), low heart rate, purplish-blue fingers and yet I would simply shake my head and say that I was fine. That was until reality hit and there was talk of wheelchairs and the hospital. The doctor sat me down and gave it to me straight.

"This is serious," he said, looking down at the papers in front of him.

"Your labs are a mess. Do you know what this means?" he asked, handing me one of the papers and pointing at my blood sugar level.

It said 32.

I stayed silent because I knew it was low . . . but I just didn't know how low it was.

He finally answered for me.

"It means that you should be in a coma, paralyzed, or dead."

That got my attention.

"But I'm not," I argued.

"And that's just because you're lucky. You might not get so lucky the next time it drops."

I vividly remember breaking down and crying. It actually did scare me, but I was just struggling so much internally that I didn't know how to help myself or how to let anyone else help me. The nurse in the room was holding me as I cried, and the doctor put his hand on top of mine. It was at that moment that I knew that they just cared, were worried, and desperately wanted to help me. I felt that they were not going to give up on me, and suddenly, I was reminded that God had not given up on me either.

This reminds me of Psalm 23:4, in which I have gotten into the habit of repeating to myself whenever I am struggling.

> Even though I walk through the valley of the shadow of death, I will fear no evil, for you are with me; your rod and your staff, they comfort me. (ESV)

There I was, followed by another looming shadow of possible death and yet God used the people around me to comfort me because He knew that I needed to be physically comforted as I was struggling to feel His presence. The staff members seemed to pour into me even more and I grew to be incredibly close to some of the nurses, especially since some of them were Christians that would even pray with me at times and encourage me with scripture.

One of the nurses would even sit with me at the table and eat what I was eating in order to help me take a bite at a time and keep my mind distracted. I also became very close with another patient who was also a believer, and we started to read our Bibles together each day.

Because of the physical state that I was in, I was woken up in the middle of the night for a two o'clock snack. Crazy, right? But apparently your blood sugar can drop while you are sleeping until it re-regulates with consistent nourishment. I also had my blood sugar checked throughout the day so that it could be treated immediately if it dropped too low.

Although I was still not eating enough, it was also due to the fact that I was still new to many meals, extremely picky with many foods, as well as how it is prepared and plated. However, I was eating more than I was before and I think everyone at the facility gave a sigh of relief, including me (mainly because that meant that I would not get sent away).

The closer that I grew with my peers and with the staff around me, the more I started to open up and accept that even if I struggled to let go of the ED and did not believe that recovery was possible . . . there were people around me that believed in recovery for me, and sometimes that was enough. In fact, everyone at the facility believed in me far more than I did in myself because as I mentioned before, we were in a teenage/young adult house and so we had school time.

The staff member in charge of education finally called me over to talk one day because she said that she was tired of seeing me roll around on the floor, bored, and essentially wasting my time. She knew that I had dropped out of college and that I had no intention of going back, however, she told me to think about going back to school online.

"It's not possible," I remember replying.

She had asked why, and I told her that it was because I lost my full-ride scholarship when I dropped out and so I no longer had the financial means to pay for school, especially with the medical bills piling up. With an understanding nod, I thought that was the end of the conversation.

BUT God.

A few days later, she pulled me over to the computer and told me to apply to community college. I stepped away.

"I told you, I can't," I said.

"I talked to your mom. She said that she would pay for you to finish college," she answered.

"What?" I asked in surprise.

She wouldn't do that. . .would she? I asked myself (it turns out she would).

"You're joking," I said.

"No," she said, shaking her head.

So, I sat down in disbelief and applied for a community college and she, my mom, and God are all to thank when I graduated with my bachelor's degree, a year and a half later. They are the reasons why I was able to finish college when I gave up all hope. However, hope never left me . . . in fact, during treatment, I named my healthy self "Hope" and the ED voice "Ed."

Naming them was a means of self-awareness that helped me to distinguish between the two voices, which one was louder in the moment, and to decide who I wanted to listen to. I truly believe that all of us have a "Hope" inside of us . . . inside of our brokenness. And not only that, but if you are believer, you have true hope living within you and God can fill you with joy and peace as we are told in Romans 15:13.

> May the God of hope fill you with all joy and peace as
> you trust in him, so that you may overflow with hope by
> the power of the Holy Spirit.

We have the hope of God, even through the broken, the darkness, and the suffering. At times we may forget, lose sight, or feel as though the light has been extinguished, however, it is still there. It is always still there.

During the holidays, treatment is a difficult time because we are away from family and loved ones, but it was especially difficult for me because I was quarantined and isolated from everyone during Christmas since the nurse I was the closest to ended up testing positive for Covid. And I just so happened to be the person that spent the most time with her and saw her last. Therefore, I was placed in my own room, and I had to participate in everything virtually. It was dreadful and when I was first put in that room by myself, I had one of the worst panic attacks I've ever had because I had never felt such loneliness as I did in that moment.

BUT God.

On Christmas day, they allowed my mom to see me, and she was even allowed to bring my dog so that I could get some dog cuddles. That gave me the strength to make it through the holidays and until the end of my quarantine.

I wish that I could tell you that the story ends here and that I completed treatment, however, my journey was still far from over and this was yet another residential treatment program that I failed to complete. In January 2022, I made an impulsive decision and another act of defiance out of fear for the future, when I ran away from the facility. A stranger found me on the side of the road and waited until staff found me, where an ambulance then took me away, off to my fourth inpatient psychiatric hospital.

I can still feel lingering feelings of regret and shame as I close off this chapter because this is the raw truth of what fear can do to you. It can make you act out in defiance to the point of ignoring the right thing and falling into sin instead. James 4:17 tells us,

> So whoever knows the right thing to do and fails to do it,
> for him it is sin. (ESV)

BUT God.

How blessed we are to be children of God! Even though we sin and have moments of defiance out of fear, God will forgive us and cleanse us from all our sins as it says in 1 John 1:9.

> If we confess our sins, he is faithful and just to forgive us our sins and to cleanse us from all unrighteousness. (ESV)

I hope that you are reminded and encouraged by His goodness and just like fear can cause defiance, it can also cause over-compliance, which I will talk about in the next chapter.

QUESTIONS TO THINK ABOUT

1. If you could change anything in your past, what would it be and why?

2. What, if any, are the desires of your heart that separate/distance you from God? Are you willing to at least consider handing them over to Him or letting Him help you to let go and grow closer to Him?

3. Who are you behind closed doors? What is the picture of yourself that you would never want to paint for others to see?

4. Was there ever a time when you were defiant out of fear? If so, how could you have invited God/others into your midst to help you react in a healthier way?

Chapter 8

Over-Compliant Fear

THERE I WAS AT another random psych hospital that had no idea how to treat someone with Anorexia. I barely consumed anything during my entire stay at the hospital, to the point of fainting. I was told by the other patients that the staff were yelling at me for sleeping on the floor until they realized it was a medical emergency. *Sleeping on the floor? In the middle of the room? Really? I'm not that crazy.*

Anyway, this was probably one of the most difficult hospital stays to get through because there were not a lot of activities or group therapy sessions provided. Mindless TV seemed to be the only entertainment. There weren't even any puzzles to do or utensils to color with! And not to mention the fact that it broke my heart that I was with a lot of patients that struggled with psychosis. This is a sad reality, however, it does not mean that they themselves are not capable of living a fulfilling life, because they are! I met people that had fulfilling lives but needed occasional medication stabilization to handle their hallucinations and paranoia.

My first day there I was having a conversation with another girl about my age, and she could hold the conversation with me, but she would also talk about things that were not there. For example, she would think that she lost her cat and would have to call for him and search for him. I cautiously reminded her about what we were talking about, and I instantly felt empathy towards her when she apologized because she would come back to herself, aware that she saw and heard things that were not really there.

And although I could not fully understand her on a deep level and what it is like to live with psychosis on a daily basis, I did know that God can, and I could relate with my own hallucinatory flashbacks and hallucination scare with my first suicide attempt. She started crying when I shared those parts of my story with her and told her that there is a God up above that sees, knows her, and loves her for who she is. Did you know that God knows the number of hairs on our head? It says so in Matthew 10:30–31.

> He pays even greater attention to you, down to the last detail—even numbering the hairs on your head! So don't be intimidated by all this bully talk. You're worth more than a million canaries. (MSG)

Don't be intimidated by the bully! The devil is the biggest bully of all, and we are far more important and loved that we do not need to be listening to all that negativity. I know that this can be hard. My mind is in a war zone most of the time where Ed and Hope are fighting each other constantly. Sometimes I wish that I could just pull them both out of my mind and set them in timeout, well, maybe not Hope. She can stay, but Ed has got to go somewhere.

Maybe I should lock him in the closet that he always shoves Hope in, but as we will find out in the next chapter, suppression will always resurface. In that case, I'll just continue to fight him with the hope that one day he will be thrown into the fiery pit of hell.

I would encourage you that when the lies of the enemy become loud, when the darkness closes in around you, or when the world bullies you, that you are reminded of just how valuable you are to God. Just as God cares for the birds of this world, how much more does He care for you? Infinitely more!

And as He sent Jesus to save us from eternal death, it is a sacrificial love that proves just how much we mean to Him. So, whether you struggle with finances, with doubt, depression, anxiety, self-criticism, or any other kind of hardship or sin, or maybe even psychosis . . . God sees you. He loves you. And He wants to take care of you. I am also reminded of the verse in Matthew 6:30.

> And if God cares so wonderfully for wildflowers that are here today and thrown into the fire tomorrow, he will certainly care for you. Why do you have so little faith? (NLT)

He created this world out of love, just as I have talked before about caring and loving your own creation. These two verses are examples of how God sees all the details and loves even His creation of the birds and flowers. There is nothing that goes unnoticed by Him as we are told in Hebrews 4:13 and Job 28:24.

> Nothing in all creation is hidden from God's sight. Everything is uncovered and laid bare before the eyes of him to whom we must give account.
>
> For he looks to the ends of the earth and sees everything under the heavens. (ESV)

When it was my time to leave the hospital, my mom and I already planned ahead that we would move to Georgia and live with my aunt and grandmother as I would continue ED treatment at a PHP day program. I dreaded yet another treatment program, especially in the secular world where they were never understanding of the importance of my faith as a part of the therapeutic process.

BUT God.

He provided me with a Christian therapist . . . in a secular setting, which is quite rare in my opinion! She spoke truth to me that I knew I was missing out on in the past year, and I started to make progress with her. We even held our own little moment where I tore up a suicide note that I had always held onto as a "just in case."

"We don't need that," she had said.

"That's just setting yourself up for failure."

She told me the raw truth that God is the only one that gets to decide when I go to heaven because Jesus holds the key to death, not me. However, as much as I was making progress in the therapeutic realm, my physical health could not keep up with me mentally. My heart, vital signs, and labs were still a cause for concern and so I was begrudgingly sent to another residential treatment center in Alabama for the spring of 2022.

I was tired.

I was frustrated.

Ultimately, I was burnt out from treatment, and I was afraid that treatment centers would dictate the rest of my life. Therefore, I made the decision out of fear, to be completely compliant, if not over-compliant. I walked into that new residential treatment facility with the mindset that I was overly committed to doing everything I was told and more. However, I took things too far. I ate more than I had to.

I supplemented extra even when they warned me not to push myself past my limit. I became movement avoidant, not participating in any physical activity out of fear that if they thought I was getting exercise and not resting to let my body heal, that I would have to stay in treatment longer. And yet, little did I know that I was setting myself up for failure in the long run.

Over-compliance is not the answer either. There needs to be balance as I've heard something along the lines of, too much of anything can also become unhealthy, even if it is technically good for you. This was true in my case. I was following the rules, but I was missing out on the bigger picture. I was forgetting the most important thing about life.

The biblical example that comes to mind is in Revelation where John is given visions from God during his exile on the island of Patmos. He follows God's instructions in writing letters to the seven churches. I can relate most to the church of Ephesus as it says in Revelation 2:2–5,

> I know your deeds, your hard work and your perseverance. I know that you cannot tolerate wicked people, that you have tested those who claim to be apostles but are not, and have found them false. You have persevered and have endured hardships for my name, and have not grown weary. Yet I hold this against you: You have

forsaken the love you had at first. Consider how far you
have fallen! Repent and do the things you did at first. If
you do not repent, I will come to you and remove your
lampstand from its place.

What a convicting revelation that even though this church
was doing so many of the right things, they were forgetting the
most important thing of all and that was the love that they had
for Christ. They needed to go back to the basics of remembering
what Jesus did for us on the cross. They needed a child-like faith
in remembering just how great and powerful our God is. They
needed to remember all that God had already done for them and
to prepare their hearts for the work that He would continue to do.

In the same way, I needed this revelation at that time, because
although I was following all the rules and exceeding expectations,
my heart was not in the right place. Just as it says in Proverbs 21:2
and 1 Samuel 16:7b, the heart is what God looks at, not what we
think we are doing right or how we appear to the world.

A person may think their own ways are right, but the
Lord weighs the heart.

The Lord does not look at the things people look at.
People look at the outward appearance, but the Lord
looks at the heart.

Even in compliance, I was struggling immensely within me.
The self-hate, distorted body image, and feelings of discomfort
intensified to the point where I completely avoided mirrors and
wore loose clothing. I suppressed the anxiety around food and the
thoughts and emotions, refusing to talk about how I was really
doing.

If I really felt unable to cope, I would find a way to self-harm.
I told God once again that I would handle this on my own. And
because I was over-complying, PTSD seemed to take over again
in what felt to be a never-ending cycle. The nightmares and flashbacks were so intense that I would sometimes be out of it for an
entire day, which was very counterproductive. I was there to heal
and yet I continued to spiral.

I lost trust in the therapist I was assigned to because she said something that was a trigger for me, and while I do not hold that against her, it was hard for me to talk to her again after that point. Trust takes time to build as we talked about in the chapter, "Breaking Trust," and sometimes in a treatment center, even a residential one, there simply isn't enough time to build that trust back once it has been broken. I ended up sticking to surface level topics, shutting down anytime she tried to dig deeper, however, I threw myself whole-heartedly into my therapy assignments and even looked forward to sharing them in group sessions sometimes.

Most of the time I would write songs on my guitar because I always brought my guitar to treatment. It was fitting that I had some training as a music therapy major because music and writing were my emotional outlets and a means of expression that I could share with my fellow peers.

As I left residential to head back to Georgia and complete the PHP program I started with, the staff expressed how proud they were of me, but also their concern for the suppression I would not let them in to help me with. I shrugged it off and did the exact same thing to make it through the PHP program. At this point, I just desperately wanted to be done with treatment and to get on with my life, however, the flashbacks hindered that. After completing the PHP program for my ED, I was sent to a PHP program that specialized in trauma treatment.

It was June 2022 when I was once again faced head on with needing to work through my trauma, but again, I was not completely on board with that. This was a unique program in which you would spend most of your time in a room, doing therapy work and assignments on your own with a therapist that would drop in to check on you and talk every so often. There were group sessions sprinkled throughout the day.

The types of therapy that they specialized in were schema therapy (identifying patterns of behavior and thought), Prolonged Exposure therapy (PE) (desensitizing fears through repeated exposure), part-work (examining different parts of self to build awareness and learning how to healthily express these parts), among other types of therapy.

Majority of our time was focused on PE therapy, where there are actually two types: in vivo and imaginal exposures. I will honestly say that I felt the urge to run and scream every single time it was brought up. I mean, who would actually want to have repeated exposure to their fears? Would you? I don't think so. If you're wondering what this looks like, I'll give you a some examples of what I was working through during in vivo exposures (directly facing real-life objects, activities, or situations that cause fear).

Walking through parking lots was extremely difficult for me because it caused extreme anxiety that led me to look over my shoulder and around me too many times to count. My therapist would walk through the parking lot with me and gave me a limit of how many times I could check my surroundings or behind me. When we first walked outside, she would ask me how I was feeling and my anxiety level on a scale of 1 to 10 and then at various times during our walk she would continue to ask the same questions.

We would only go back inside after my anxiety level decreased and I became aware that there was no immediate threat or anything dangerous about the parking lot. And as scary as it was to me in the moment, this type of therapy was actually quite helpful because I can make it through a parking lot today, still with a bit of anxiety, but not to a debilitating point of total avoidance.

Something else that I was working on is quite vulnerable because I was afraid of knives, and yes, that is linked to my trauma history. It started with just looking at the word, then at pictures, and then at a real one. The same questions were applied here, and I had to look at those things until the anxiety level decreased to a tolerable state and although knives are dangerous, they are not something to be afraid of to the point of never wanting to see or touch one. I also made significant progress here, where I am now able to help my mom in the kitchen by chopping up vegetables and using the knife as a tool.

So, Prolonged Exposure therapy (PE) falls under the umbrella of Cognitive Behavioral Therapy (CBT), which works on self-awareness and the changing of destructive thought patterns. Many of the past treatment centers I have already talked to you about focused mainly on CBT; Dialectical Behavioral Therapy (DBT), which focuses on emotional regulation, distress tolerance, and living in the present moment; or Acceptance and Commitment Therapy (ACT) that works on lessening self-judgement and becoming more accepting of thoughts and feelings. If all the therapies that I mention to you just go over your head, that is completely okay! It can be a lot; however, I mention them just so you have an idea of what is out there in the mental health world.

As I continued with PE therapy, imaginal exposures were my worst nightmare because you are vividly remembering your traumatic memories and directly confronting the fear you feel as a result of them. This meant purposely going into a flashback for me, which never ended well for anyone. I was not able to make any progress in this area, and I was becoming increasingly exhausted.

Eventually, my mom and I decided that I would not complete the treatment program because we were going to move back to Texas in August of 2022 so that I could go back to college in person. The treatment center disagreed and said that I needed more help, but I left anyway and moved on, accepting that I might never be completely healed from the trauma inside.

BUT God.

Today, I am still in trauma therapy and continuing on my healing journey, however, I firmly believe that I stand on the other side.

QUESTIONS TO THINK ABOUT

1. How often do you thank God that He sees you, knows you, and loves you for who you are? What steps can you take to develop a heart of gratitude? Think about starting a gratitude journal and writing down 3 things every day that you are thankful for.

2. Have you ever told God that you would take care of things yourself? How did that turn out for you and what could you have done differently?

3. Have you ever thought that you would not be able to heal from something? What would it be like to hand that over to God and completely trust in His plan for your life?

4. Do you or have you struggled with over-compliance out of fear? If so, how might you surrender that fear to God and ask Him to help you respond appropriately?

Chapter 9

Resurfaced Suppression

SUPPRESSING MY THOUGHTS AND emotions through the distractions of life became as easy as drinking water. If anything, it was a flashback to the past. I moved back to Texas where my mom and I lived in an apartment. I had just started the fall semester of college and a new job with a private babysitting company. I got the opportunity to babysit for multiple families, however, it was draining to drive all over the Dallas-Fort Worth (DFW) area to different houses.

I was enjoying my classes and even got a music therapy practicum placement at a local children's hospital because I was aspiring to work in a children's hospital as a future career. However, I would have to face another sad reality that this was not God's plan for me.

I continued therapy in the outpatient world, but I did not find someone that I truly connected with. In fact, I left each session feeling worse about myself than I did when I went in. The saying is right when they say that finding the right therapist is much like looking to buy a car. It takes time, as does many things in life.

At first things were okay until one of my therapists believed that I struggled with BPD in addition to all my other struggles, however, she would blame me for the emotional dysregulation and behavior instead of seeing it as a disorder that needed time and patience to work through. In October 2022, she sent me to my fifth psych hospital, especially because October was a very difficult month for me ever since my first suicide attempt. Luckily, my mom bailed me out again and I took a break from therapy for a while.

I thought that everything would be okay, however, my music therapy professors started to have conversations with me that left me confused about my future. They started to question if I was in the right profession and if I was ready to become a therapist if I had not yet healed from my own trauma and struggles. It hurt to acknowledge that they were probably right and that it was not the right time for me to pursue a music therapy career. It was not that they did not believe in me, because they definitely did and said that they would always welcome me back with open arms when I was ready to complete the program, however, my circumstances at the time clearly showed me that I was not ready.

At my practicum placement at the children's hospital, I was told to work with a teenage patient that had just attempted suicide. I was immediately reminded of my own attempts, and as you can imagine, I could not do it, or I did not feel ready to. I completed the practicum with what I could do, but at the end of the year, I had a difficult decision to make.

I was told amazing news that I secured a music therapy internship at a mental health private practice in Florida, when I was looking into my other options for graduation. My heart broke when I told the internship director that I had to decline her offer because I was changing my major for spring 2023 to graduate early.

She was so understanding, and I did end up explaining my situation to her, in which she said that if I ever went back to the music therapy world, I still had a place with them. That meant more to me than she would ever know. This is similar to the grace of God because even in moments where we walk away, He still reassures us that we ALWAYS have a place with Him. As it says in Titus 3:7,

> So that being justified by his grace we might become heirs according to the hope of eternal life. (ESV)

How comforting is our reminder of eternal life with Him and the fact that we are adopted into His family as heirs. There are many verses in the Bible that reassures us of this promise, and because it is hard to decide which ones to include, I have provided a few of my favorites to hopefully act as a reminder to you when you are in need of comfort and to remember that you are a preciously cherished, beloved child of God.

> What marvelous love the Father has extended to us! Just look at it—we're called children of God! That's who we really are. But that's also why the world doesn't recognize us or take us seriously, because it has no idea who he is or what he's up to. But friends, that's exactly who we are: children of God. And that's only the beginning. Who knows how we'll end up! What we know is that when Christ is openly revealed, we'll see him—and in seeing him, become like him. (1 John 3:1–2 [MSG])

> Now you are no longer a slave but God's own child. And since you are his child, God has made you his heir. (Galatians 4:7 [NLT])

> I will be a Father to you, and you will be my sons and daughters, says the Lord Almighty. (2 Corinthians 6:18 [NIV])

> But to all who believed him and accepted him, he gave the right to become children of God. They are reborn—not with a physical birth resulting from human passion or plan, but a birth that comes from God. (John 1:12–13 [NLT])

For the spring semester of 2023, I put on my mask again of perfectionism and people-pleasing and did my best to hold myself together. I continued to suppress everything, ate what people expected of me, and avoided movement as much as possible because I was trying to make sure that I would not get sent back to treatment.

However, at the start of the summer semester, I slowly started to slip without even realizing it. Suppression was not working anymore, and I was oblivious. My breakfast became smaller and smaller until I stopped eating it altogether. The snacks slowly started to disappear as well, and the other meals grew smaller in size.

As I mentioned before, I was oblivious . . . either that, or I was straight up in denial again. The reality of my situation did not hit me until around the time I graduated college in August 2023. My mom and I were at a public market for the annual watermelon festival when I began to feel dizzy. I walked cautiously, hoping my mom did not notice that I was bracing myself on tables and anything in my path because I was also short of breath and my heart was racing. We were waiting for my mom's order of dumplings when my vision went black, and I fainted.

I woke up to my mom wiping my face with a cold washcloth and paramedics hovering over me. They took me into the ambulance to further check up on me.

"I'm not going to the hospital," I said.

"Why?" one of the paramedics asked.

"I'm just not going," I replied.

"What was the last thing you had to eat?" the other one asked me.

I paused for a moment.

"Watermelon and green tea."

The paramedic closest to me made a face.

"That's a bad combination."

I laughed but then refused to tell them anything else other than the fact that I was fine and just wanted to go home. So, they reluctantly let me leave once my vitals calmed down. However, I had to face my mom, and she sat me down really quick.

"You're relapsing, aren't you?" she asked.

"I don't know," I shrugged.

She just gave me that sad look and begged me to eat some of her dumplings. I only took a few bites and that was that. Suppression through distractions in life was not enough to hold me together, and so I did what I knew best . . . I let myself fall into the deep hole of starvation. I fell back into the enemy's hands and let Ed lock Hope away to take full control. I am about to share with you a poem that I wrote many months later because I think it gives a clear picture of the extent the enemy can go to in order to try and destroy you. He takes your weakness, whispers lies, and tempts you until you no longer feel like resisting.

This poem is the depth of my brokenness. Here is . . .

WEIGHT OF A RELAPSE: A POEM OF PAIN-FILLED TRUTH

It starts with whispered lies . . .
ones you've heard before.
You're able to ignore . . .
until the voice grows cold.
Colder than before.
Meaner than before.
And yet you want control, to numb the pain, to distract from reality.
So you cave.
You give in.
Even when you know the consequence.
The reflection in the mirror becomes a blur, a distorted image, a liability.
You've lost too much weight.
Too fast, too quick.
You see it, but you don't.
And that voice tells you it's not enough. . .
"keep going," it whispers . . .
And then maybe, just maybe, you'll be enough.
People comment, push the diet mentality, adore you even . . .
Some out of fear and concern.
Some out of oblivion.
Either way it's triggering.
And they've got no clue.

It starts with restriction, that's your go-to behavior . . .
the one that's most familiar . . .

along with a spiral of calorie counting, food rituals, measurements, body checking, daily weighing, and throwing out food in a panicked frenzy.

I tear my food.

I take small bites.

I eat in order . . . by color, size, whatever . . .

No crust on bread.

I separate my plate.

No foods can touch.

Sometimes I even chew and spit, as much as I'm embarrassed to admit.

Or I excessively drink water, chew gum . . .

anything to make sure hunger doesn't linger.

I cut out food groups.

I avoid the kitchen like the plague . . . restaurants and fast food too, or at least I try to.

I definitely don't cook.

I wear loose clothing when I'm uncomfortable.

And oh, don't forget about dieting . . .

I've tried pretty much every single one seen in advertising.

I'm obsessed with the numbers:

Calories.

Nutrition labels.

Serving size.

BMI.

Weight.

Circumference.

Steps.

It's exhausting . . .and I hate math.

You'd wonder why I do it.

I've got no clue . . . other than, I'm obsessed with the numbers.

And just when I didn't think it could get any worse . . .

I'd go a week without eating.

Extreme hunger sets in . . .

which leads to a "binge . . ."
well, my idea of a binge.
So then I try to purge . . .
Even when It's an intense fear . . .
But I'm desperate.
And a few times it worked
which left me passed out or crying on the floor.

I'm so desperate I pull diet pills off shelves, engage in laxative
abuse, diuretic abuse, and my body hurts . . .
But I'm desperate.
The image in the mirror is a blur, and for some reason, I hate her.
She feels unlovable.
Unworthy.
Broken.
Fragile.
The trauma broke her.
And it doesn't feel like anything will get better.
A hopeless mess, looking back in the mirror.

Overexercise comes back stronger than before:
I do sit-ups in bed.
Planks, crunches, my abs must always be in pain.
I've got bruises, carpet burns on knees and elbows . . . I pace and
stand when I can.
My hips, knees, sides . . . everything hurts when I walk . . . and yet
I push myself beyond measure.
My joints pop if I move too fast.
My feet have blisters from all the steps.
Those numbers climb higher and higher . . .
And I ask myself what I'm doing to myself,
But you see . . .
I'm desperate.

I fight the weight restoration process.
I refuse to go to treatment.

It doesn't work anyway when you're not ready.
You have to want it.
You have to embrace it.
You have to accept it.
And I'm not there yet . . .
Even as I feel myself growing weaker.
Even as I feel my body struggling.
Even as I faint, feel dizzy, or my vision blacks out when I change positions.
Even as my hair grows thinner and thinner, clogging up my shower drain.
Even as I always shiver, my body unable to control its temperature.
Even as I'm always nauseous, needing a heating pad, or laying on my stomach.
Even as I'm told my thyroid has issues, or my blood sugar is low, or I have several nutritional deficiencies . . .
somehow my brain just can't comprehend when enough is enough and it hurts.

Even as the suicidal thoughts return.
Even as my mood swings leave me even more confused about the highs and lows.
Even as it is hard to sleep, it hurts to sleep . . . or as it hurts to sit in a chair, especially if it's hard because I can feel my bones everywhere.
Even as I cry almost daily . . .
an embarrassing amount over food or my body.
Even as I question why I do it.
Even as I fight with my family,
just about eating.
Even as I avoid special events,
just to avoid eating.
Even as I ditch my order at a fast food restaurant because I panicked last minute.
Even as my dog found pepperoni, hiding in my closet because I hate people seeing me eat.
And he totally exposed me.

Made me feel vulnerable.
Made me feel weak.
Made me feel uncontrollable.
But who's to blame, but me.
Even when you know the consequence . . .
You give in.
You cave.

Anorexia knows your weakness.
It knows your secrets.
It knows how to push your buttons.
It knows what lies you'll think you believe.
It makes you lie to your treatment team.
It knows you hate looking in the mirror.
It makes you hate your very being.
It knows your pain.
It knows you want to distract and escape.
It knows you want . . . no, need control.
It makes you spiral out of control.
It knows your name . . .
and brings you shame.
This is the weight of a relapse . . .
one that kills you slowly.
But I'll fight it every day,
if it's the last thing I do.
I can only pray.

When I wrote this poem . . . things became real. The weight of my sin became unbearable, but I felt as though recovery was hopeless for me. My weight felt unbearable even though I was technically underweight. It didn't matter. I still wanted to shrink until the outside of me, matched the inside. I wanted to shrink into oblivion, to become completely invisible, to not exist anymore. Just like trauma is stored in the body . . . the reflection of our outer selves, is very much a reflection of what is on the inside, whether you are aware of it or not. And whatever you suppress, will resurface eventually.

In my story, suppression was quite evident in my outward appearance, but I was tricked by the enemy into thinking that I was still functioning. The more I obsessed about calories, weight, all things ED related, the further I could squash the traumatic memories, unwanted thoughts and feelings until I was a numb shell, walking through the motions in life as though I were a living zombie.

What a miserable way to live if you really think about it . . . and I wish I could go back in time and make myself see it. Just as Eve was tricked by Satan in Genesis, we are told in 2 Corinthians 11:3 that our devotion to Christ may become corrupted just like sin was brought into the world in the beginning.

> But I fear that somehow your pure and undivided devotion to Christ will be corrupted, just as Eve was deceived by the cunning ways of the serpent. (NLT)

So, what then can we do in order to save our faith and our hearts you may ask. Well, it starts with surrender and humility as you must release what you are suppressing to God. You have to let go of it because as I was once told by a wise person in my life . . . it is impossible to have one foot in the world and one foot in Christ.

There is only one or the other because either God has your whole heart . . . or He does not know you. This is a choice between life and death. Deuteronomy 30:15–20 is a long passage to include, but I believe it is so important for us to read and remember because it lays out our choice, clear and direct.

> Now listen! Today I am giving you a choice between life and death, between prosperity and disaster. For I command you this day to love the Lord your God and to keep his commands, decrees, and regulations by walking in his ways. If you do this, you will live and multiply, and the Lord your God will bless you and the land you are about to enter and occupy. But if your heart turns away and you refuse to listen, and if you are drawn away to serve and worship other gods, then I warn you now that you will

certainly be destroyed. You will not live a long, good life in the land you are crossing the Jordan to occupy. Today I have given you the choice between life and death, between blessings and curses. Now I call on heaven and earth to witness the choice you make. Oh, that you would choose life, so that you and your descendants might live! You can make this choice by loving the Lord your God, obeying him, and committing yourself firmly to him. This is the key to your life. And if you love and obey the Lord, you will live long in the land the Lord swore to give your ancestors Abraham, Isaac, and Jacob." (NLT)

Although the time of the Israelites is very different from the times we live in today, the choice is still the same, but we must believe in Jesus to have life, and naturally, our love for God will follow. I am currently being discipled by someone that God lovingly placed into my life at exactly the right time, and we have been going through Deuteronomy. To help you process and understand this passage further, I will explain how we have been applying Deuteronomy to our own lives.

The promised land could be thought of as heaven, but it should also be thought of as a place that we get to in our lives on earth that are filled with peace and joy no matter the circumstances. It is when we are spiritually mature enough to run to God whenever we are troubled and to rely on His strength and power to get us through this life. It is when we are using our spiritual gifts to glorify Him and when we worship Him with praise from a humbled, grateful heart.

On the other hand, the enemies and giants that the Israelites face are our internal struggles, sins, and brokenness inside that hold us back from fully trusting God. It could be the enemy himself and the lies that he tempts you to believe. It could be the people around you that discourage you and fill you with doubt. It could be your own inner self-critic and insecurities.

Whatever they may be, know that you have a choice. I pray that you choose life and live it to the fullest with all that God has in store for you. It will be a choice that changes you from the inside out and it will be a blessing beyond anything this life could possibly offer you!

QUESTIONS TO THINK ABOUT

1. Think of a time when you suppressed thoughts or emotions. Where were you? What were you doing? Why did you feel the need to suppress instead of express?

2. How did suppression work out for you? What were the consequences, if any?

3. Have you ever walked through the motions of life, feeling like a zombie? Maybe you were depressed, sleep deprived, or grieving. How were you able to "wake up" from that state of being?

4. What does your "promised land" on earth look like? What are the enemies and giants that are holding you back from a fulfilling life?

Chapter 10

Broken Beyond Repair

"I CAN'T WATCH . . ." MY mom started to say, crying to me one day.

I knew what she meant. She did not have to finish the sentence. I was wasting away, and she didn't want to watch me die, especially not from starvation. I remember that I was curled up on the couch where I sat each day, too weak and dizzy to do anything. I was so numb that I barely felt any emotion as my mom cried over me. I could not even feel the pain I was causing her, and I simply closed my eyes to will the world away. *I guess this is my life.*

BUT God.

He would not let that be my life.

There was a small part of me, the Hope within me, that was screaming in the far-off distance. She was crying and begging me to let her out. As much as I tried to ignore it, that day, I couldn't stand hearing her screams anymore.

"Okay," I said, opening my eyes.

"I'll go back to treatment."

However, I was very unhappy about my decision and had already internally planned to make sure that everyone around me knew that I clearly did not want to recover, and I was only doing it so I could stop hearing their cries. I had agreed to treatment, not to recovery. It was selfish, self-sabotaging, and another one of my most shameful moments. I had forgotten one of the most valuable lessons my mom taught me growing up. She would sing me a song every morning before school that was based on the Bible verse, Romans 12:21.

Do not be overcome by evil, but overcome evil with good.

I had given the enemy a foothold, not necessarily meaning to, but falling into the trap he laid out for me. In a way, I stepped right into it when I refused to hand over the ED to God. I was at church one time, asking for prayer, when one of the ladies asked me,

"you're holding onto something, aren't you?"

I asked her what she meant, and she described something very profound to me. She said to imagine myself standing in a box of God's presence, where I know Him and His goodness and His blessings. Then she told me to hold my arm out as if I was carrying a bag in that hand.

"That hand is holding onto something outside of God's presence. Something that you don't want Him to have," she said.

I had to blink back tears.

"I can't," I told her, shaking my head.

And I'll never forget what she told me as I walked away that night.

"You will," she said.

In September 2023, I ended up at an ED residential treatment center in California where they only treated six patients at a time. We were in a small, cozy house that overlooked a valley, and we would often watch the sunset out in the backyard. I would end up spending both Halloween and Thanksgiving there.

As is typical for ED treatment, our meals and snacks were at the same time each day and there were therapy groups mixed in between. Individual therapy was twice a week and so was the meeting with your dietician. In the evenings, we got to have our cell phones and any other electronics, including TV, and, on the weekends, they would take us on an outing which would include the beach, a mall, a random store, a park, or to pet and feed the llamas that lived in our neighborhood.

Every week, a different client was chosen to cook a meal for everyone with the help of the dietician and the chef on staff. We had yoga twice a week, played Just Dance or played outside sometimes for our mindful movement group, and walks could be approved. I was even allowed to watch a church sermon virtually every Sunday morning. It was probably my best residential treatment experience despite the fact that I fought the process immensely. *Not again . . . right? I should have learned my lesson.*

Yet there I was refusing to complete even half my meal plan again . . . in fact, I did not complete my meal plan the entire time I was there until the very last week, and that was only because I wanted to save face and embarrassment for being discharged without complying with my treatment plan. That's what happens when you refuse help and are not committed to recovery. Not only that, but I just struggled a lot with how far away I was from my mom and her family . . . literally on opposite sides of the U.S. That seemed to intensify the number of nightmares and flashbacks that I had, and it took a while for the facility to learn how to best help me through those.

The fear and anxiety related to trauma increasingly worsened to the point where I could not go on outings unless a therapist went with me. I also self-harmed almost daily until they started wrapping my entire arms so that I could not scratch myself. It was so embarrassing, but I did understand that they just cared and were looking out for my well-being. I would disassociate almost every group session, to where the days blurred, making me feel as though I weren't really there. I was just a ghost, following everyone around and hiding in the corner. Whenever I could, I would be off to the side, puzzling, collaging, or writing a song on my guitar.

BUT God did bless me with incredible peers where I am still quite close with one of girls I met there because she is also a believer, and we would sometimes watch church together on Sunday mornings. I was also blessed to have gotten close to many of the staff members where I still keep them updated on my whereabouts in life today.

God also blessed me with the first therapist to ever tell me that I could work on the trauma at the same time as the ED. She's the one that helped me to see that it did not have to be this never-ending cycle where trauma treatment would send me to ED treatment, which would then send me back to trauma treatment, and you get the picture. The cycle would never end.

I was lucky to have her, because I truly believe that if I did not, I would have been sent to another trauma facility. I say this because there was a day when my therapist was not there, that I had a flashback that lasted for hours, and another staff member told me that it might be better for me to go to another facility that was better equipped to handle my case.

I broke just hearing that because to my ears, that meant that I was not wanted and that no one would ever be able to help me. It made me feel even more broken than I already was, and so in desperation, I spiraled even deeper into darkness. Out of another impulsive decision, fueled by fear, I stole a bottle of pills from the nurse's station and ran with them.

BUT God.

He did not let me get far.

I ended up shaking and crying in the driveway, where I was taken to my sixth psych hospital. I thought that I knew fear better than anyone, and yet, the fear that I felt at the hospital was a fear that was crippling beyond what I had felt before. I was uncertain about my future and situation because I was miles away from my loved ones and unsure if the residential treatment center would take me back into their care after all the trouble I had already caused them.

BUT God.

I will keep saying it time and time again because He did SO much for me, especially throughout the story in this chapter and the next.

It was a struggle for me to eat at the hospital and I barely consumed anything, however, the psychiatrist that I was assigned to was also somehow a psychiatrist on staff for the same treatment center where I was at for residential, just at a different location. That could have only been God.

There was no way that she just so happened to treat eating disorders at exactly the same treatment center in addition to the job she already had at the psych hospital. And because she knew what she was doing, she knew that I needed to get back to the residential facility as quickly as possible, however, we had the issue of how I was going to get back because I was an hour away.

BUT God.

My therapist at the residential facility personally drove to pick me up, showing me yet another moment where God's love and care overwhelmed me.

"You came to get me," I told her, in shock.

She smiled.

"Of course, I take care of my clients," was something along the lines of her reply.

And although I was still struggling with my faith, I remember feeling God's love in that moment. It was a warm presence that reassured me that everything would be okay. Even though I was miles away from my loved ones, He was still with me and was providing me with people to shower me with love. As it says in Joshua 1:9 and Psalm 46:1, I could have ran from East to West or as deep as the depths of the sea, BUT God would still be with me and He would always be there to help me in times of despair.

> Have I not commanded you? Be strong and courageous. Do not be afraid; do not be discouraged, for the Lord your God will be with you wherever you go."
>
> God is our refuge and strength, always ready to help in times of trouble. (NLT)

Throughout the rest of my time in California, I developed a unique relationship with my therapist because she had gained my trust in more ways than simply picking me up from the hospital, but she showed that she truly cared for me. She would take me on a walk to help keep me present as I talked about things I had never told anyone. She held me as I cried when my mom told me over a zoom call that one of my aunts was dying. She would dump colored pencils and art supplies on the ground and scatter puzzle pieces all over the facility so that I could use my organizational skills as a distraction instead of self-harming. She let me rip up much too much grass in the backyard to help ground myself.

She was definitely creative in her means of therapy and that will mean more to me than she will ever know. She challenged me and I made some progress, however, not enough to where we knew that if I was not going to embrace recovery, then there was nothing more to be done.

I was given a discharge date; however, I would not be allowed to leave on my own due to not being trusted with my own medications and my flashbacks were also so intense that they were not sure I would be able to make it through an airport by myself. I started to panic, worried that I would have to be away from my family and stay in California longer for the PHP and IOP programs there.

BUT God.

My loving mother flew from coast to coast just to get me and that was another moment of time, that when I was able to finally throw my arms around her, I did not want to let go. It was another God moment where I was shown an overwhelming amount of love. And as I said my goodbyes, my therapist said,

"see you in 3–4 months."

I think my mouth dropped open before replying.

"I won't be back," I said, shaking my head.

Some say that it was insensitive for her to say that, and it was, but she was making me face reality. She knew me well enough to where she knew I needed to hear the possible consequence of my decision. By not choosing recovery, I would indeed end up in treatment again or worse off than I already was, and unfortunately, I was stepping down to a PHP program in Texas where I did continue to decline because of my unwillingness to let go of the very thing destroying me from the inside out.

If you can guess, I struggled with the same things at the day program, having flashbacks almost daily, disassociating in groups, and barely eating anything. I was often the last one sitting at the table after each meal as staff tried to encourage me to eat, but it was no use and if anything, I was annoyed that they were trying to help.

"I don't want your help," I would often say, until one day, I got a response that I was not expecting.

"If you don't want our help, then why do you keep showing up every day?"

I think my heart hardened even more in that moment. I wish that it hadn't. I wish that God would have saved me from the road this was leading me on. I wish that I had not put my body through what I did. I wish that I could go back and scold myself for not thinking rationally. I wish that I did not continue to break myself. I wish that I was not someone that had to learn things the hard way. I wish that I could have avoided rock bottom. I wish . . . I wish . . . and yet it does not do well to dwell on wishes. I know that God had a reason why He let me go through what I did. He knew that I had to see and experience it for myself if I was ever going to embrace how He truly wants me to live this life.

And so, at the beginning of January 2024, I went home that day, e-mailing that I would not be back to the program, and leaving AMA. I broke beyond repair, or so I thought at the time, because for the next few months, I spiraled to a point that I did not think I could ever come back from. I literally hit rock bottom.

BUT God.

He provided for my every need, even when I told Him I did not need Him.

He never stopped loving me, even as I hated my very being.

He comforted me, even when I pushed Him away.

He pulled me out of darkness, even as I was drowning.

He forgave me, even as I couldn't possibly think of forgiving myself.

And most of all . . .

He never gave up on me, even as I fought Him.

I am reminded of the verse in Psalm 34:19–20, where it says that God protects and will deliver us from all our troubles, even the ones that you do not think you could ever come back from.

> The righteous person may have many troubles, but the Lord delivers him from them all; he protects all his bones, not one of them will be broken.

My days looked the same as I continued to walk through life, zombie-like for many months. I was lying to my treatment team and pushing people away that tried to make me see reason that the ED was hurting me. I was lying to myself that everything was fine and that I was in control.

However, it was a false sense of control. It is always a false sense of control because when you think that you're the one in control, more often than not, the enemy is actually the one in the driver's seat. Control is not something that we should be seeking on this earth. It is true that the Bible tells us to have self-control in the fruit of the spirit, however, true self-control is shown out of humility, not out of pride.

So, as I continued in my brokenness, thinking there was no way out, today, I hope to remind you that there will be a day that all brokenness will be gone. There will be a day where there is no more suffering and pain. There will be a day where we will no longer think that we are broken beyond repair, because ultimately, we are not. We know of the ultimate healer. May we meditate on the verses Romans 8:18 and Revelation 21:4–5a that remind us of the glory to come.

> For I consider that the sufferings of this present time are not worth comparing with the glory that is to be revealed to us. (ESV)

> He will wipe every tear from their eyes, and there will be no more death or sorrow or crying or pain. All these things are gone forever. And the one sitting on the throne said, "Look, I am making everything new!" (NLT)

QUESTIONS TO THINK ABOUT

1. Is there anything that you are holding onto outside of God's presence? Are you willing to ask God to help you release it to Him or to help you take necessary steps in order to do so?

2. Do you feel a need for control or seek to control certain aspects of your life? How might you begin to release that control to God?

3. Have you ever felt broken beyond repair? What would it be like to be honest with God and ask Him to help you believe that He is capable of healing?

Chapter 11

Hitting Rock Bottom

I smile. I cry.

I laugh. I scream.

I blink . . . and there is a war that rages on in my head.

No one expects the unexpected—when our world collapses in on itself and rock-bottom smacks us right in the face.

BUT God.

It was in April 2024 that I woke up surrounded by wires . . . uncomfortable, in pain, incredibly weak, and startled by the alarm that was going off above me. A nurse ran in just as I tried to crane my neck and see what was making all that racket. I blinked. *That couldn't be right.* I blinked again, trying to refocus my eyes. The nurse pushed some buttons and sighed. I was able to see it clearly that time. I took a deep breath and tried to speak. My voice came out shaky.

"That's not my heart rate, is it?" I asked, just as the nurse headed for the door.

She turned.

"Yes, and it is only at that number because of the IV medications going into you . . . otherwise, it would be a flat line."

She left.

The cold response made me shiver, or maybe it was because the room was physically cold . . . either way . . . fear froze my heart because my heart was beating at less than twenty beats per minute. I could feel it. The beats were inconsistent. My heart was struggling, both physically and emotionally.

I was dying.

That was not my intention. I did not want to die . . . I only wanted the pain to end. That is what most people struggle to understand . . . so let me continue to explain and summarize what we have already discussed throughout this book.

Over time, the pain that I feel from trauma and abuse is suppressed as I try to harness a false sense of control and put on a mask that "everything is fine" so I will not be an additional burden to others. However, there is only so long that I can pretend and continue to suppress my feelings. As I have said before, eventually, they will bubble to the surface, whether you want it to or not.

This is exactly what happened in the spring of 2024, but the decline of my health started many years prior, as you witnessed throughout my story. I thought that I had control. I thought that everything was going well. You see, this is exactly what the enemy wants you to think. First Peter 5:8 says,

> Be alert and of sober mind. Your enemy the devil prowls around like a roaring lion looking for someone to devour.

You may think that you have control. You may think that things are going well even . . . but as 1 Thessalonians 5:17 says,

> Pray continually.

The devil will find a way to use your weaknesses against you. My weakness is mental illness, and you may, or may not be able to relate in this aspect, but we all have hardships and struggles. It is part of the human condition where we are lured into traps and fed lies on the daily.

And as I fell into the trap and lies . . . I thought that because I had such a blessed community and support system that nothing could possibly go wrong. I was deceiving myself with the enjoyment of life with all the adventures of travel and opportunities. I thought that I could hold it all together. I was lying to myself, telling myself that I was doing all the right things to be healthy, when in turn . . . I was destroying myself. I was choosing death. I was ignoring God.

As God talked about the people of Israel in Jeremiah 32, verse 33 depicts how I was treating God . . . I was breaking His heart.

> They've turned their backs on me—won't even look me in the face!—even though I took great pains to teach them how to live. They refused to listen, refused to be taught. (MSG)

As I looked at my reflection in the mirror through rose-colored glasses, the enemy whispered lies to convince me that what I was doing was good . . . He deceived me into turning my back on God and continuing on the path of destruction, thinking that I was doing the right thing. I thought that the diets were healthy. I thought that the exercise regiments would make me strong. I thought that diet pills were just supplements. I thought that comparison would just push me to be a better person. But the enemy took it further than that . . .

One diet turned into multiple, which then turned into eating nothing at all for a week at a time.

One exercise program turned into multiple, which then turned into an obsession that left blisters on my feet and bruises on my back, elbows and knees.

One bottle of diet pills turned into multiple, which then turned into the abuse of diuretics and laxatives.

What I initially thought to be harmless . . . went to the extreme. I will remind you that this is how the enemy works. He takes a small argument and blows it up out of proportion so that it becomes a fight. He takes a small feeling of insecurity and lowers self-esteem to the point of severe depression or anxiety. He takes a small compliment and entices someone to become overwhelmed with pride. He takes a small mistake and destroys all that he can. In John 10:10, Jesus tells us that,

The thief comes only to steal and kill and destroy; I have
come that they may have life, and have it to the full."

That is the hope within. Although we fall and go through trials of suffering, as believers, we are reminded that Jesus says in
John 16:33,

I have told you these things, so that in me you may have
peace. In this world you will have trouble. But take heart!
I have overcome the world."

I am a living, breathing, miracle today because of God's grace
and because Jesus overcame the world and death itself. I will quote
Revelation 1:18 once again, where Jesus says,

I am the Living One; I was dead, and now look, I am
alive for ever and ever! And I hold the keys of death and
Hades.

The day that God miraculously saved me from death, started
like any other day. I followed my routine and crossed things off
my to-do list. I thought that I felt a little off, but I shrugged it off
as I went to the park to overexercise and fed the urge to reach an
insane number of steps for the day. That is where I panicked. I felt
my walls start to break. I felt the darkness fight and crawl for the
surface. My mind very quickly became a chaotic war zone. I dialed
a friend's number.

She answered.

". . . but I'm not going to do anything stupid," I remember
telling her after rambling on about my internal struggles.

She listened, encouraged, and sent love and support my way.

I hung up, but I didn't feel any better and so I dialed another
friend's number.

She texted.

"Is everything okay?"

I texted back that I was fine because I decided not to bother
her, and I continued walking. It was almost time to head to my
church for a recovery group meeting anyway.

By the time I got in my car to drive to church, it felt like a gray cloud had settled over my head. I started to feel emotional pain creeping back up to where I had to remind myself to breathe. I started to remember some of the trauma that happened to me. I did not want to feel or remember and so I asked God,

"why?"

No response.

I managed to make it into the church where my mentor embraced me in a hug and asked how I was doing. My walls came down. The pain, sadness, anger, and a swirl of all other negative emotions flooded me. I cried.

"Like I shouldn't be here," I told her, but I should have been clearer.

She reassured me that I belonged at the church and encouraged me to stay for the evening, even if I had to cry the whole time. So that is exactly what I did. I curled up on a couch in the corner and cried my heart out, but I didn't feel any better. Instead . . . I felt unheard. I felt abandoned. I felt lonely. Again . . . all lies from the enemy.

As I got in my car to drive home that night . . . it felt like the weight of the world fell upon my shoulders and I no longer had the energy to fight. I clenched my chest as I cried because the emotional pain was unbearable. I was exhausted and so I thought the only way out was to go to the extreme. I begged God to take me home to be with Him, but I took matters into my own hands . . . again, thinking that I could be in control.

I was far from control . . . I was spiraling out of control. My mom was sleeping in the room next to me when I attempted to take my life that night . . . but the moment that I overdosed, I instantly regretted it. Tears ran down my face and I told God over and over that I was sorry but that I just couldn't do it anymore. The pain was too much to bear. Fear seized me and I texted some close people in my life . . . but I should have been clearer, because I was essentially saying,

"goodbye."

As I laid my head down to sleep that night, I told God that I would either see Him soon, or maybe He could miraculously save me again, because this was not the first time something like this had happened as you know by now . . . and you would think that I would have learned my lesson.

BUT God had a reason.

He did not give up on me.

I laid in bed and begged Him to save me because I didn't want to die. I knew I had made a mistake. My phone rang. My hands were shaking as I reached for it. Tears continued to fall as I answered it. *How did she know? She doesn't check her work phone after hours . . .* It was my therapist.

"What did you do?" she asked, but not in a demanding way.

Her voice was kind and filled with concern.

I broke.

God used her to hear me that night, when before, I felt unheard.

My mom took me to the hospital in time for me to collapse into a wheelchair and get sick in the middle of the ER waiting room. Nurses immediately took me back and I barely remember anything else.

God used my mom to let me feel cherished as she held me, when before, I felt abandoned.

I was placed in the Intensive Care Unit (ICU) and the doctors told my mom that they didn't think I was going to make it. They were trying to prepare her. Anorexia had done more damage than we knew, and the overdose was the last straw.

My heart was failing and could not support itself, needing a PICC line directly to my heart.

My liver was failing.

My kidneys were failing and there was talk of putting me on dialysis.

My stomach could not hold any food down.

My blood sugar was unstable, causing me to need insulin shots or to be treated for low levels.

My labs were a mess, completely depleted of electrolytes causing me to need potassium, magnesium, phosphorus and other fluids and medications added to my IVs.

My blood pressure was always too low.

My mind was hallucinating cats and fake doorways.

My body was so weak that I was bedridden, and I was told,

"you will die if you do not start to eat. The IVs cannot keep you alive forever."

I share this not to scare you or for pity . . . but to emphasize how close I was to death and the magnitude of God's power to pull me back from the brink of death.

He is miraculous.

He is powerful.

He is merciful.

He saves.

Throughout my time in the hospital . . . I felt Him. I could feel Him holding me. I felt His love for me, and I just knew that everything would be okay. Even as I had to use a walker in physical therapy because I was too weak to walk. Even as I had to have help to the bathroom because I had orthostatic hypotension and would pass out. Even as I cried over food because I still felt the need to starve. He was there and He never stopped loving me. Romans 8:35–39 says,

> Who shall separate us from the love of Christ? Shall trouble or hardship or persecution or famine or nakedness or danger or sword? As it is written: "For your sake we face death all day long; we are considered as sheep to be slaughtered." No, in all these things we are more than conquerors through him who loved us. For I am convinced that neither death nor life, neither angels nor demons, neither the present nor the future, nor any powers, neither height nor depth, nor anything else in all creation, will be able to separate us from the love of God that is in Christ Jesus our Lord.

Nothing.

Absolutely NOTHING.

Nothing can separate you from God's love as a believer . . . not even death.

As I fought for my life, I was showered with God's love not only from Him, but through an incredible amount of support from my mom, friends, and church family.

God used my loved ones to help me feel supported, when before, I felt lonely.

They held my hand. They held me. They prayed over me. They cried out on their knees. They interceded for me. They pleaded for my life.

God heard my cry.

God heard their cries.

Isaiah 65:24 says,

> Before they call I will answer; while they are still speaking I will hear."

God answered before I even cried out to Him.

God answered while my loved ones were still praying.

This was the hardest fight of my life. I was faced with the reality of what I had done to my body. I was faced with the reality of what I put my loved ones through. I faced God and the consequence of my suppression, fear, doubt, and all the things that I held onto, outside of His presence.

Once I was medically stable enough, I was transferred to my seventh psych hospital where I continued to experience God's love and care. I felt my heart soften and in the back of the ambulance during my transfer, tears rolled down my face in a moment of immense regret and shame. I cried out to God.

"I'm sorry," I whispered to myself and to Him.

I wrapped my arms around myself, knowing that I still had to walk the healing journey, and it would not be easy. It never is. Today, I still have my ups and downs. I go through scary periods where I think I may relapse again. I still have nightmares and flashbacks sometimes, but I am doing the therapy work. I still have moments of doubts and questions, but I seek God and people to point me back to Him. Sometimes I even take back that false sense of control, only to be reminded of where that path leads, knowing I must let go.

During that psych hospital stay, I embraced recovery and allowed the people around me to guide and help me on my journey. The doctors helped to continue monitoring my health and the dietician helped to get my body back on track with consistent eating. My peers were a source of encouragement as I met other believers, and God already started to use me in that dark place, but not before testing my renewed faith.

There was a day where a Bible study was being held on a Wednesday night, however, they had a movie night planned for the same time. I kept watching the clock, especially when they started the movie, and everyone gathered in the main room. *That couldn't be right.*

"Isn't there Bible study tonight?" I asked one of the techs.

"Oh, yeah, but I figured no one would want to go since we have a movie playing," she said.

"But I want to go," I said.

"Oh," was her reply, before telling me that she could not take me to it because it was about to be shift change.

I nodded in defeat and went to sit back down. However, I was restless inside. It was as if I knew the enemy was trying to keep me from something I needed to hear that night. So, I waited until shift change was over before asking another staff member. She waved me off and said that she had to take care of something.

I could feel my frustration rising, but if you know me . . . you know I have a strong-will. From a young age, my mom said that anytime I set my mind to something, I would always see it through. And just recently, I had a therapist ask me,

"What would it be like to use your strong-will for recovery instead of for your detriment?"

I will never forget that question, because it has changed everything. And at that instance in the psych ward, I continued to persist and ask different staff members until I found someone that would take me even though I was almost thirty minutes late. But that was okay. I did not give up and I made it there in time to hear that God would use my story. I heard that God would use my past. I heard that God would use my brokenness. He had a plan. Just as it says in Jeremiah 29:11,

> "For I know the plans I have for you," declares the Lord,
> "plans to prosper you and not to harm you, plans to give
> you hope and a future."

As much as I wish this hardship never happened . . . it is part of my story, and I can confidently say that what man intends for evil . . . God turns into good. The example that I think of in the Bible, is the story of Joseph. He had been sold into slavery by his brothers and even ended up in prison for a crime he did not commit.

However, what man clearly intended for evil . . . God turned into good. Joseph ended up becoming second in command to all of Egypt as God blessed him with the gift of interpreting dreams and he was able to interpret the dreams of Pharoah, who promoted him above all others. Joseph tells his brothers in Genesis 50:20,

> You intended to harm me, but God intended it for good
> to accomplish what is now being done, the saving of
> many lives.

In my life, what the devil had intended for evil . . . God also turned into good. If I did not experience what it means to hit rock bottom, I would not have come to a point of submission to fight to let go of the eating disorder and to finally embrace the recovery journey. I would not have the desire to live life to the fullest and experience all that there is to offer. I would not have the passion to share my story with the world, to inspire, and to share the creativity God has gifted me with to give Him glory.

QUESTIONS TO THINK ABOUT

1. Do you wear an "everything is fine" mask? If so, how might you take a step towards letting down the walls and being honest with yourself and maybe even someone else?

2. What weaknesses might the devil be trying to use against you?

3. What would it be like for you to use stubbornness or a strong will to do what is right instead of for harm? How much more will God be glorified?

4. Do you have examples in your life of "what man intends for evil . . . God turns into good"?

Chapter 12

God Uses the Broken

TOWARDS THE END OF my time in the psych hospital, I was in group therapy one day where we were given pieces of paper that looked like the front section of a car. There was the front windshield above the dashboard which took up majority of the paper, but at the top, there was a rearview mirror. We were told to write or draw what we were looking forward to in the windshield and then what we wanted to leave behind in the review mirror. I knew what I had to write . . . *but was I ready?* I would never be ready.

BUT God.

Unlike other types of recovery—like for addiction or alcohol, where the answer is abstinence—for an eating disorder, there is no clear answer for recovery. Food and fears must be faced every single day. We live in our bodies, uncomfortable and learning how to tolerate those feelings. There is no escaping the body we live in. There is no escape from food, especially in a culture that is centered around food and the fact that we need it to survive. Recovery is a choice that must be made every single day. I knew what I had to write. I knew I had to surrender it. I knew I had to let go completely.

At the end of group, we each had to go around and share. I could feel the anxiety rising within me, because it is one thing to write something down on paper, but it is made real when you speak it out loud into existence. When it was my turn to share, I started with the fulfilling life I was looking forward to, especially since I knew that my mom and I were about to officially move into our own apartment in Georgia that summer to be closer to her family. It would be a fresh start that we truly needed. It would give me a reason to move on. It provided me with hope, and as I finished sharing, I ended with,

"I'm leaving behind my eating disorder."

To my surprise, a girl in the back corner of the room spoke up.

"I wish I could write that on my paper," she said.

I froze for a moment, but the peace of God washed over me. I gave her a small smile and said,

"you can . . . just please don't wait too long like I did . . . I almost died before I made that decision."

Since then, there have been many new moments of freedom and joy! Of course, healing takes time, and the ED is not completely gone, but it is much quieter and does not have the control that it used to have. Recently, I have even started praying daily that God will continue to give me the strength to fight each day and care for my body.

I pray that I respect my body for what it does for me and that one day I can even love and cherish it for who I am made to be. I pray that one day, the thoughts and fears disappear with time to where I am fully recovered and completely free. The verse that keeps me most rooted in ED recovery is found in Matthew 6 when Jesus teaches on not dwelling on worries. Verse 25 says,

> That is why I tell you not to worry about everyday life—whether you have enough food and drink, or enough clothes to wear. Isn't life more than food, and your body more than clothing? (Matthew 6:25 [NLT])

The answer is an astounding, YES! Life is SO much more than that! Think of all your loved ones, the beauty of nature, or all the adventures and opportunities that life brings. Beauty is brought forth from ashes, and as I moved forward into a new life, I was reminded of a visual imagery a therapist once had me imagine. However, it did not really connect with me until I embraced recovery for what it was.

I was told to imagine that my past trauma, pain, and regrets were all wrapped up in a glass ball that I had to carry with me, wherever I went. You could see the painful memories replaying themselves if you looked into the glass. I was then told to imagine that I had a meeting with Jesus, but I was reluctant to go because I was ashamed that I carried a glass ball with me. However, He came to me and reached out His hand for the ball. It was then my decision to either trust Him with my brokenness and give the ball to Him, or to walk away, still holding onto it.

This was where I was always stuck. I was always hesitant, and I always saw myself walking away . . . that is until recently. I can finally picture myself handing that ball over to Him, and He takes it from me lightly, but then throws it to the ground and shatters the glass. It is a shocking revelation, because as the glass glitters around us, He embraces me as the whirlwind of my life swirls around me and He does not let go. The swirling storm continues throughout this earthly lifetime, but Jesus is the eye of the hurricane where peace and calm resides.

This is what it is like to let go of suppression and to no longer be hiding and pushing things down, deep inside. The memories may never leave, and your story is still a part of you . . . BUT God holds onto you, and He will never let go. Just as God promised Jacob that He would always be with him, in Genesis 28:15, I believe that God promises that to us too, as we see in many other verses and stories throughout the Bible.

> Behold, I am with you and will keep you wherever you go, and will bring you back to this land. For I will not leave you until I have done what I have promised you."
> (ESV)

God has surely fulfilled many promises throughout my life, and with a fresh start in Georgia, I have been blessed beyond words to describe. God has poured into me and shown me His patience and love as He has surrounded me with a church community and many believers that encourage and strengthen me. I have made so many new friends that point me back to Jesus. I am in a season of life where I can use my talent for God's glory.

I have had new opportunities to promote my debut book, *Transforming Tears*, which tells the life story of my grandfather. I am even in a relationship for the first time, learning to lean on and trust God throughout more healing that is still to come. As I know that there will still be trials and tribulations, I hold tight to the word of God as we are told instructions for living, such as in these verses:

> You were taught, with regard to your former way of life, to put off your old self, which is being corrupted by its deceitful desires; to be made new in the attitude of your minds; and to put on the new self, created to be like God in true righteousness and holiness. Therefore each of you must put off falsehood and speak truthfully to your neighbor, for we are all members of one body. "In your anger do not sin": Do not let the sun go down while you are still angry, and do not give the devil a foothold. Anyone who has been stealing must steal no longer, but must work, doing something useful with their own hands, that they may have something to share with those in need. Do not let any unwholesome talk come out of your mouths, but only what is helpful for building others up according to their needs, that it may benefit those who listen. And do not grieve the Holy Spirit of God, with whom you were sealed for the day of redemption. Get rid of all bitterness, rage and anger, brawling and slander, along with every form of malice. Be kind and compassionate to one another, forgiving each other, just as in Christ God forgave you. (Ephesians 4:22–32)
>
> Be joyful in hope, patient in affliction, faithful in prayer. (Romans 12:12)
>
> Let the peace of Christ rule in your hearts, since as members of one body you were called to peace. And be thankful. Let the message of Christ dwell among you richly as

you teach and admonish one another with all wisdom through psalms, hymns, and songs from the Spirit, singing to God with gratitude in your hearts. And whatever you do, whether in word or deed, do it all in the name of the Lord Jesus, giving thanks to God the Father through him. (Colossians 3:15–17)

I include these long passages because I believe in their importance for how we should strive to live this life. I believe in the importance of meditating upon them and asking God to help us live a Christ-like life and to be an example for those around us, even amidst our pain and brokenness.

For in my brokenness, I can share with others how the POWER of God healed me.

In my darkness, I can share that God was the LIGHT that led me back to life.

In my regrets, I am a witness of God's FORGIVENESS.

In my shame, I am an example of how the GRACE of God covered me.

In my rock-bottom moments, I was shown the depth of God's LOVE, able to share it with others.

God uses broken people. We see that throughout the Bible where David was a man after God's own heart and yet he committed adultery and was an accomplice in murder. Jonah tried to run from God and acted out in defiance and rebellion. Peter lived in fear and denied knowing Jesus. Paul persecuted and murdered Christians. Thomas doubted. Jeremiah was depressed and Elijah may have been suicidal. And yet, God used each and every one of them to do His work, and if He used them, He will certainly use YOU, for as it says in Matthew 5:3–12,

Blessed are the poor in spirit, for theirs is the kingdom of heaven. Blessed are those who mourn, for they will be comforted. Blessed are the meek, for they will inherit the earth. Blessed are those who hunger and thirst for righteousness, for they will be filled. Blessed are the merciful, for they will be shown mercy. Blessed are the pure in heart, for they will see God. Blessed are the peacemakers, for they will be called children of God. Blessed are those who are persecuted because of righteousness, for theirs is the kingdom of heaven. Blessed are you when people insult you, persecute you and falsely say all kinds of evil against you because of me. Rejoice and be glad, because great is your reward in heaven, for in the same way they persecuted the prophets who were before you.

In fact, God wants to use broken people because His LIGHT shines all the more brightly in the darkness. His GOODNESS is most clearly seen through moments of despair. His GLORY is exemplified in our suffering. His STRENGTH holds us together in moments when we should be falling apart. His POWER is displayed for all to see through the brokenness we experience. As we are told in 2 Corinthians 12:9,

> But he [Jesus] said to me, "My grace is sufficient for you, for my power is made perfect in weakness." Therefore I will boast all the more gladly of my weaknesses, so that the power of Christ may rest upon me. (ESV)

It may sound crazy to boast about weaknesses but think about how inspiring it could be for others to see how God worked in your life through those moments of weakness. Think about how much of an impact your story could have. We may have freedom in Christ; however, the healing journey is still lifelong. There will still be moments of weakness, temptations, and tribulations. There will still be challenges and difficulties because this earth is not our heavenly home.

My family is actually walking through a very dark time right now as my parents just divorced because my father is marrying someone younger than me . . . yes, you read that correctly . . . he is marrying someone five years younger than his own daughter . . . and my mom and I never thought we would ever need to reach out to a domestic violence program and yet here we are in the protection of one.

I never thought that feelings would resurface and that I would have to humble myself and forgive my father all over again. And yet, that is what it means to be human. Just as Jesus commanded us to forgive 77 times as in Matthew 18:21–22, and that does not mean literally, but to repeatedly forgive as God has covered our sins. Whether it is the difficult task of forgiveness, or fighting temptations, be reminded that Jesus takes on our burden for us and we are not alone as we trek through life, known as the "valley of the shadow of death," mentioned in Psalm 23:4.

As we fully surrender our whole heart to Jesus and make Him Lord over our lives in all areas, and as we continually forgive those that we need to forgive, over and over again . . . a release is felt within as we embrace God's peace and presence. As we humble ourselves in repentance, we draw closer to God and shine His light for others to see. As we walk in faith and not by sight, we discover our identity in Christ and live our lives according to His will, holding tight to Him in the midst of struggles.

My reason for sharing my story and hardships, not only here, but on social media and on my blog, is so that I can hopefully bring more awareness to mental illness and start conversations, however, it is also ultimately to bring God glory and share with others about His overwhelming love for us. I have a story to share, and I have a hope within that I do not want to keep quiet if it could potentially help someone else!

Throughout my new season of life and even amidst continued challenges, I have heard from God in more ways than one, not just from the people around me, but because He continues to do amazing things. For example, in a time of need at Bible study one evening, two of the ladies gave me the very same passage of scripture that they felt God lay on their hearts. Not long after, someone else in Bible study quoted it again, and after that, it was given to me by my significant other.

It did not stop there, as the verse continued to be brought up in conversations, there was the most miraculous moment of all . . . I was looking through my closet for something to wear when I found a sweatshirt from a woman's retreat I had attended in the past. I had no recollection of the fact that we had studied that same passage during our time at the retreat, because it was quoted on that sweatshirt. *No way!* If you're wondering what this passage is . . . it is Lamentations 3:19–25.

> I remember my affliction and my wandering, the bitterness and the gall. I well remember them, and my soul is downcast within me. Yet this I call to mind and therefore I have hope: Because of the Lord's great love we are not consumed, for his compassions never fail. They are new every morning; great is your faithfulness. I say to myself, "The Lord is my portion; therefore I will wait for him." The Lord is good to those whose hope is in him, to the one who seeks him.

If you have not read Lamentations, I would encourage you to do so. I had not read it until I was given this passage, but I was surprised that this book of Jeremiah's brokenness and despair was included in the Bible. Surely, that means that God truly cares about our suffering. He wants us to be honest with Him about how we are really feeling, just as David gives us a beautiful example through all the Psalms he wrote.

David was authentic in His worship to God about where his heart was at, and God wants that depth of a personal relationship with us. In our moments of struggle and doubt, may we take our thoughts and feelings to God and sit in His presence as we are on this earth, because our present suffering will never compare to the glory that awaits us. Romans 8:17 tells us

> Now if we are children, then we are heirs—heirs of God and co-heirs with Christ, if indeed we share in his sufferings in order that we may also share in his glory.

Just as Christ suffered, we too will suffer in this life because if we truly acknowledge it for what it is . . . this world is beyond broken. We are beyond broken.

BUT God.

We are His children, and He loves us beyond comprehension.

We will be with Him in eternity one day where there will be no more suffering or pain.

We are and will be blessed in too many ways to count.

If you allow Him . . . He will use your brokenness for good.

He will use your suffering to do His work and mighty deeds.

He will use your story to bring Him glory.

He will make beauty from ashes.

He will instill hope within.

Because beyond a shadow of a doubt . . . we can see that hope lies within the broken.

QUESTIONS TO THINK ABOUT

1. What are your "BUT God" moments? How can you give Him thanks and glorify Him today?

2. If you were to do the activity that I did in group therapy, what would you write in the windshield to look forward to, and what would you put in the rearview mirror to leave behind?

3. Imagine that you had a glass ball of your past and all your pain and regrets . . . would you hand it over to Jesus, or would you walk away thinking you still needed to hold onto it?

4. What would it take for you to believe that God can use you despite your brokenness? How can you take a step today, to be used for the kingdom of God?

Acknowledgments

MAY ALL THE GLORY be given to God in guiding my hand and giving me the words to write in this book. May He get all the glory for my story as I share it with the world and tell you of His goodness. May I always seek Him not only in seasons of joy, but in seasons of suffering and sorrow. I hope that this book will be a reminder to myself of the healing journey I walk, and all that God has brought me through. I do not even have the words or the feelings to express the amount of gratitude I have in my heart that God saved me from near-death so many times. He gave me many second chances when many people don't get that, and that is the ONLY reason why I am alive to tell my story today.

Many thanks also needs to be given to my main support, my role model, my best friend, as God blessed me with the most wonderful mom. She has been with me through it all and I also do not have the words to express my thanks to her. I put her through so much, but just like God never gave up on me . . . she did not either and she cared for, loved, and prayed over me throughout not just the past few years . . . but my entire life. Mom, I love you beyond words to describe!

I would also like to thank all the people I met on my journey, whether that be the staff members of hospitals and treatment centers, to other patients and their loved ones, as well as my own treatment team and support system. I will also name a few people who have been in my close circle throughout the years because I do not want the amount of support and love that you gave me to go unnoticed. So . . . Darin, Brianna, Kat, Rebecca, Izzy, Molly, Rylie, Mila, Denise, Leslie, Melissa, Susan, Christine, Herani, Latoria, both Amandas, both Sarahs, and both Danielles, I say thank you today for the role you played in my life, whether that be accepting and loving all of me, to pointing me to Jesus and believing in me. From the bottom of my heart . . . thank you!

www.ingramcontent.com/pod-product-compliance
Lightning Source LLC
Chambersburg PA
CBHW060359090426
42734CB00011B/2194